IS ELVIS REA[L?]

NO!

Says Myrna W., who sold a piece of her handmade craftwork in upstate New York to a familiar-looking mystery man who told her he was buying it for "Lisa."

NO!

Says Joyce X., who warned the renter of a secluded cabin in Florida to beware of over-inquisitive tourists—and was rewarded with a note of thanks . . . signed **"E.P."**

NO!

Says Devon L., who was joined in song on a deserted Illinois street by a man claiming to be the King—before the stranger was whisked away in a black stretch limo.

NO!

Says a stunned crowd in a Louisiana honky-tonk, rewarded with an impromptu set by Elvis Presley—who then disappeared as suddenly as he had arrived.

THE ELVIS SIGHTINGS

PETER EICHER

AVON BOOKS NEW YORK

THE ELVIS SIGHTINGS is an original publication of Avon Books. This work has never before appeared in book form.

AVON BOOKS
A division of
The Hearst Corporation
1350 Avenue of the Americas
New York, New York 10019

First Avon Books Printing: August 1993

AVON TRADEMARK REG. U.S. PAT. OFF. AND IN OTHER COUNTRIES, MARCA REGISTRADA, HECHO EN U.S.A.

Printed in the U.S.A.

RA   10   9   8   7   6   5   4   3   2   1

For Lisa.
Contra Mundum.

CONTENTS

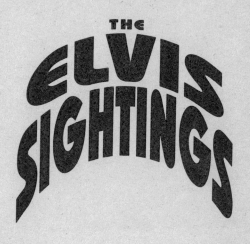

PROLOGUE

It was the afternoon of August 16, 1977, a hot, ninety-four-degree day in Memphis. Charles Crosby and Ulysses Jones, paramedics for the Memphis Fire Department, were going through their typical day.

A call came in: Alert. . . . someone having difficulty breathing . . . proceed to 3764 Elvis Presley Boulevard.

Crosby and Jones knew right away: the address was Graceland, the home of the King. They suspected that the person in trouble was Vernon Presley, Elvis's father, whom they had helped before when he suffered a heart attack. Surely, Vernon was again the victim. It couldn't be the King. Not Elvis.

It was 2:32 P.M. when the ambulance headed for Graceland. By 2:48 it left, traveling at speeds of over eighty miles per hour. Seven minutes later it arrived at Baptist Memorial Hospital. The patient was rushed inside to a waiting medical team, and for half an hour doctors worked feverishly, using all the techniques available to them. But it was no use. The patient died. The case was officially declared a Dead On Arrival.

Even while the doctors worked, rumors were flying. Reporters monitoring police broadcasts picked up the call for an ambulance to Graceland. Speculation was running wild: Was it Elvis? Was the King the one rushed to the hospital? The press descended on the hospital like locusts, buzzing around everywhere looking for a story, awaiting any word from the medical staff. Finally, it came, and when it did it confirmed everyone's worst fears.

The reporters were called together and told. Yes, it was Elvis Presley. He had died that day, at 3:30. A heart attack seemed to be the cause. Later that night, the medical examiner gave an official press conference and confirmed that the cause of death had been "cardiac arrhythmia," an erratic heartbeat. The man who had broken so many hearts, and filled so many hearts with joy, lost his battle with life when his own great heart gave out. The irony seemed bitter and terribly unfair. But few were thinking of such things at the time. It wasn't time for contemplation; it was time to mourn together as a family.

And so they did. By the thousands, they came to Graceland. Only two hours after Elvis's death was announced, three thousand fans were outside the gates of Elvis's mansion, sharing their grief. The crowd continued to swell. It seemed limitless, inexhaustible. Over the course of the next day, more than eighty thousand people came, from all parts of the country. This wasn't the death of a singer, or a rock and roll star. This was a death in the family, the largest family in America.

Flowers poured in by the thousands. They threatened to overwhelm the grounds. So many flowers were sent that the city of Memphis ran out! Five tons worth of emergency supplies were sent in from Colorado and California. Never had anyone been so mourned. Messages came in from around the world. President Carter issued an official statement from the White House. The governor of Mississippi declared a day of mourning, and the governor of Tennessee had all flags lowered to half-staff.

Prologue

When the gates were opened for people to pay their last respects, over twenty thousand passed the coffin in three and a half hours. That was all the time allowed. Thousands and thousands more were left waiting outside. No photographs were permitted, yet one appeared.

And here begins the real story.

Only one photo was taken of Elvis in his coffin. It was published in the *Enquirer* and has been published elsewhere since. Yet the picture is a curious one. Elvis is lying deep in his coffin. Only the top of his face can be seen, in profile, about up to his ear. No other part of his body is visible. His face seems surprisingly young and unblemished. Where is the heavy undertaker's makeup, the grisly look of the embalmed? The medical examiner had claimed there was a full autopsy, yet there seems to be little swelling of the face, though people on the inside claim he was grossly swollen. Why the contradiction between story and photo? For years, these questions and many others went unanswered and, perhaps, largely unasked. But eventually, nearly ten years later, there would be an answer. Many would not believe it. Some would scoff, others would laugh. But something was going on, something incredible.

On August 16, 1977, the world was told that Elvis Presley was dead. On that very same day, the greatest mystery of our time began.

IS ELVIS DEAD?

Is Elvis Presley, the greatest musical entertainer of all time, truly dead? The question is simple. The answer is a mystery.

It is easy to scoff, at first. After all, his death was reported in every newspaper and on every television station in the free world. Literally hundreds of news reporters descended on Graceland by the end of the fateful day. Could they all be wrong? Were they all duped into believing that Elvis was dead, when in truth he lived? It seems crazy, too farfetched even to consider for a moment. Crazy, yes, until you start to take a careful look.

This book contains no proof that Elvis Presley is alive. Yet it contains no proof that he is dead. There are no verified, hundred-percent certain stories of people having seen Elvis. Yet there is no proof that they didn't. What we have is what this book presents: some conjecture, some curious facts, and many stories from many people.

Truth is sometimes hard to come by, but belief isn't. All of the tales of Elvis sightings are true to the people involved. A few may have doubts, but most are unshakably convinced that they have seen Elvis Presley, and that they have seen him after he reportedly died. Many have spoken to him, some at great length. It is their stories that make up the greater part of this book.

Because of the sensitive nature of this issue, in most cases we have not revealed people's names. Too often in the past, people who have seen Elvis have been deluged with phone calls and letters, harassed by news reporters and investigators, hounded by scoundrels somehow trying to cash in on the memory of the King and the loyalty of his fans. To avoid such exploitation, we have respected their privacy. However, the stories themselves are as close to the truth as we could make them.

LOOKING FOR
THE FACTS

There are several theories about what actually happened on August 16, 1977. Some are more convincing than others, yet there are interesting aspects to all of them.

The central idea, on which most of the major investigators of this issue seem to agree, is that Elvis Presley faked his death. There are differences about how he did it and why, but one thing is beyond dispute: it is an unsettled issue. There are too many loose ends, too many strange details, and too many people who have seen Elvis alive to shrug off the question any longer.

One suggestion, not taken very seriously by most but still worth mentioning, is that Elvis did die, and the inconsistencies surrounding his death resulted from the fact that he was murdered. This might explain a few seemingly out-of-place facts, but it certainly doesn't account for all the people who have seen Elvis. We feel safe in our conclusion that whatever happened, Elvis was not murdered.

So then why do some people think Elvis is alive? There is no single reason, no major clue, but rather a collection of facts and conjectures. Some of them are admittedly minor, but brought together they build up a convincing case that the whole truth of this matter has not been revealed.

To begin with, there are contradictory stories about the way Elvis supposedly died. It is unclear when his body was found, or who found it. The "official" story was that Elvis was found dead in his bathroom, yet there are variations concerning the exact location of the body at the time it was found. Supposedly, Elvis was reading a book when he died, yet some sources claim it was a book about the Shroud of Turin, which Elvis was known to be interested in, and others say it was a book about astrology, another interest of his.

As one follows the events of August 16, more and more suspicious details emerge. When Elvis was taken to the hospital, a nurse is reported to have said to another nurse, "That's not Elvis Presley. Who is this, nurse?" The nurse making the statement knew Elvis and had dealt with him on previous occasions.

Contradictory stories have emerged about the details of the autopsy. Larry Geller, a longtime friend and hairstylist for Elvis, described the autopsy incision as an X-shaped cut. Autopsy incisions are almost always T-shaped. Why the improper procedure? Furthermore, Geller styled Elvis's hair for his funeral, and he claims there were no marks on Elvis's head and nothing unusual about his hair. Others contend that parts of Elvis's hair, particularly his sideburns, had been pasted on. This would not be unusual after an autopsy, because the top of the skull is normally cut off so samples of the brain can be analyzed. Often this damages the hair, which has to be replaced either by gluing on the original hair or using fake-hair patches or a wig. Clearly, different people are claiming to have seen different things, and they cannot all be correct.

The events surrounding the funeral are also curious. Vernon Presley personally called several Elvis Fan Club presidents and requested that they not attend the funeral. He claimed that it would be too hard on them emotionally.

He also told Elvis's secretary of many years not to attend for the same reason. All of these people knew Elvis well, yet they were specifically told not to go to the funeral. Could it have been because Elvis was not dead, and the body at the funeral was not the body of Elvis Presley? Were these people, so close to Elvis for many years, too likely to notice something was wrong?

Elvis's coffin presents more questions. It was a huge coffin, weighing over nine hundred pounds. Such coffins cannot be purchased overnight. They have to be made to order, and it takes quite some time to manufacture and ship them. Yet the coffin was available for the funeral only two days after the "sudden death." This is a plain impossibility. No amount of money could have made the coffin available that quickly. It must have been ordered in advance. This suggests that the "death" was planned.

Some people who believe Elvis faked his death also feel that he left behind certain quiet clues for his loyal fans. There are two such clues. One is that his middle name is misspelled on his grave. The gravestone spells Elvis's middle name, Aron, with two A's: "Aaron." This could be a simple mistake given that the name is most often spelled with two A's, yet why has it never been corrected, over fifteen years later? Some feel it is a sign that whoever is in that grave—if, indeed, there is anyone at all there—is not Elvis Aron Presley.

The other clue is a curious number quirk. In the last several years of his performing career, Elvis would begin his shows playing the bombastic Richard Strauss composition *Thus Spake Zarathustra,* a tune made famous by its use as the theme music to the science fiction film, *2001: A Space Odyssey.* Indeed, the music is most commonly referred to simply as "2001," which has become the name most people know it by. And if you take all the numbers of Elvis's death date—August, the eighth month, on the sixteenth day in the year 1977—and add them together, the total comes out to 2001. A coincidence? Perhaps, but there are only twelve days in any given year that possibly add up to 2001. Only one day in each month will add to that precise number. There is less than a four-percent chance of this happening at random. So was it a fluke occurrence, or was it a carefully planted clue, an indication that the day of the "death" was precisely calculated and planned well in advance?

If one accepts, even for a moment, the possibility that Elvis did not die, and that he faked his death, the next logical question is how did he do it? If Elvis never died, whose body was in the coffin at the funeral? There are two schools of thought on this issue.

One school claims that the "body" in the coffin was, in fact, a wax dummy. This may seem laughable to some people, but anyone who has been to a good wax museum knows how remarkably lifelike wax replicas can be. In addition, the only known photo of Elvis in his coffin shows so little of his face, and not very clearly at that, that it could well be a wax figure. What adds to the mystery is the fact that photographs were strictly forbidden at the funeral. The photograph that appeared was reportedly taken secretly and "smuggled out" by a poor relative of Elvis. Is this story true, or is it a clever cover-up? Pretending that the picture was taken without approval would only make it seem more genuine. It becomes the picture that "they didn't want taken." Human nature, being suspicious, would lead most of us to believe the picture *was* real precisely because it was unauthorized. How easily we believe anything that appears to be a "dirty secret." How clever to use our suspicion against us.

Such theorizing may be convincing, but there is a far more direct reason for the wax dummy hypothesis: somebody said so. Elvis impersonator Sammy Stone Atchison was at Graceland, along with thousands of other Elvis fans, on August 17, 1977. While there, he spoke to David Loyd, a cousin of Elvis. Sammy claims that David told him this remarkable story: "When you see the white hearse tomorrow, Elvis won't be in there. It is a wax dummy. The real Elvis is leaving in another hearse tomorrow night.''

So was this the plan? Put a dummy in Elvis's place and sneak him out the next day, a day when nobody would pay any attention to a hearse because they thought Elvis was already buried? Again, if this was all carefully plotted, the plan consistently relies on a keen understanding of human behavior. Who would bother to look inside a hearse *after* a funeral? Who *wouldn't* believe an "unauthorized" picture? Every step shows great calculation.

Now we need to return to the nine-hundred-pound coffin. Why was it so incredibly heavy? The answer falls into place now: the wax replica of Elvis had to be kept cool. If it started to melt during the funeral, the jig would be up. So the coffin contained a cooling unit to keep the wax at a reasonable temperature. If you've ever tried to lift an air conditioner, you know how heavy such cooling units are. It was precisely this that added so greatly to the weight of the coffin.

Furthermore, there are eyewitness reports that state Elvis's face had beads of sweat on it at the funeral. When asked this, Joe Esposito, Elvis's longtime road manager, replies that the air-conditioning at Graceland broke on that hot August day, and everyone was sweating. That answer is acceptable only if you don't know anything about what happens to a dead body. Any undertaker will tell you that after death the sweat glands in the body are completely shut off. In addition, by the time of the funeral the body has been drained and filled with embalming fluids. It is plainly impossible for a dead body to sweat, no matter how hot the air is. But if you've ever taken a cool can of soda out of the refrigerator on a hot summer day, you've seen beads of condensation form on it almost immediately. What, then, would happen to a wax figure being cooled by secret refrigeration units when it is brought into a warm, sticky room? Condensation. Of course, if you don't know it's a wax figure, it looks like sweat. Was this an unseen flaw in the carefully laid plans?

While inconclusive, the wax dummy theory is certainly worthy of consideration. It could work, if someone wanted to try it. But there was a simpler method available.

This is the second school of thought on how Elvis faked his death. Put simply, it could be summed up this way: "Why use a dummy when you can use the real thing?" The "real thing" is not, of course, Elvis Presley, but an impostor. Not Elvis, but a real human body.

This brings up an ugly possibility. Was someone murdered to provide a substitute for Elvis? No one seems to think this was the case. It is too much out of character for Elvis, who would never agree to killing someone so he could "escape." But there are some who believe that there may have been a look-alike who was dying of some kind of terminal illness. The person may have agreed to the deception. It is simple enough to imagine that in exchange for the Presley estate's paying for his medical care, he would bequeath them his body. Perhaps it was someone who wanted his family taken care of and agreed to allow his body to be used if his family was provided with a large sum of money. There are as many possibilities as you can imagine for such a thing to happen without resorting to killing anybody.

Assuming this was the case, the funeral arrangements would have been prepared well in advance. This would allow for the large coffin to be ready so quickly and it would have allowed Elvis to leave Graceland before the death was announced, before hundreds of reporters and thousands of people swarmed into Memphis.

There is one curious piece of evidence in support of the impostor idea. Numerous reports claimed that Elvis was bloated at the time of his death. Even reports before the death suggest that. Yet one of the bodyguards who worked for Elvis the last few years of his life has said that while Elvis had put on some weight, he was in no way bloated.

12

However, an impostor undergoing harsh medical treatments or suffering some awful disease may well have been in a bloated condition. One could even wonder if Elvis was trying to put on weight to look more like the man he knew would be bloated at death.

There is one simple way to prove or disprove the impostor theory: exhume the body buried at Graceland. Dental records would provide positive proof if it is Elvis who is buried there. But it will never happen. The Elvis estate has made it more than clear that there is no possibility of this happening. It would require a court order, and that would only be obtainable if there were solid evidence of foul play. There is no such evidence, so the body will remain where it is.

Either theory, the wax dummy or the impostor, is plausible in its own way. Either one could have worked. We can't say which was used, or even which seems more likely to have been used, but both scenarios point to some unexplained curiosities. Why are there contradictory stories about Elvis's appearance at his death? How was the coffin built so quickly? Why did some people see sweat on the body? These questions and others have no answers, but there must be answers. The truth must lie somewhere in between all these questions.

There is another important question as well. If Elvis faked his death, why did he do it? What reasons did he have for taking such an incredible step? We will consider these questions in a later chapter. For now, let us turn to the most important people in the great Elvis mystery: the people who have seen him alive. It is time to hear some of their stories.

WHAT STARTED IT ALL

Of the numerous Elvis sightings there have been, perhaps the most famous is that of Louise Welling of Vicksburg, Michigan (near Kalamazoo). Indeed, it was Mrs. Welling's story, which first broke in 1988, that started a wave of people coming forth and claiming that they, too, had seen the King.

Though it is clear that some of the accounts that appeared after Welling's were frauds, her story is far more compelling. Indeed, she has no doubts about what she saw.

"I have seen him. I don't *think,* and it wasn't an impersonator. I think I have all my faculties. I did see him. He's living here."

In fact, at the time she said the above words, in July of 1992, there had recently been another indication that Elvis Presley was spending time in the Kalamazoo area.

"About five weeks ago now, my mom had heard on her television set that they had an Elvis sighting. I called [the TV reporter] and asked if it was true, and she said yes.

They have a police scanner at the station where they heard the news, but it wasn't confirmed yet.

"A week after that my husband and I and my two teen-age daughters were listening to my police scanner. It was around seven in the evening and this officer came on and said 'I'm checking into the presence of Elvis.'

"We all heard it. He had to be in the area."

Upon hearing such information, many people wonder why Elvis Presley would be in the Kalamazoo area. Most people think of Elvis as a Southerner and expect he would be in Tennessee or Alabama or some other Southern state. But Louise Welling has an answer to such doubts. She has kept her eyes and ears open over the years, and she has put together an intriguing collection of facts.

"When Elvis came to Kalamazoo for the first time [for a concert in 1973], he made some comments to the audience that he had a friend in Michigan. He also mentioned knowing someone in Vicksburg. And I have found out through checking some certain things that he had relatives that lived in Michigan that owned a motel. So he does have ties to Kalamazoo."

The facts continue.

"When my husband and I were first married we used to get the Galesburg *Argus* [a small newspaper] that tells what's going on and so on. It was September of 1973, and I happened to see in the *Argus* that Elvis Presley would be at the Columbia Hotel in Kalamazoo. It gave a date of the twenty-fifth but it never said why or what reason. See this was about the time my daughter Vicki was born and I remember that. And when he came to Kalamazoo for the first time I didn't go see him then because I had just given birth. I really wanted to check it out and I thought to myself, now why isn't that in the Kalamazoo *Gazette,* the big paper. I found out he had to know someone who lived in Galesburg to have put that in there.

"Remembering that, when he came to Kalamazoo in 1976, I called that hotel and I said could you tell me if

Elvis Presley will be staying there. The young lady that answered the phone said yes, he is, and did I know that the manager was a friend of his. So he does have connections here. He definitely has connections to Kalamazoo.''

Clearly, Mrs. Welling has established reasons why Elvis Presley would be in the Kalamazoo area. With both relatives and friends in the area, what better place to go if he wanted to remain anonymous? Who better to trust with his secret than people he knew well?

Already, Louise Welling has made an interesting case. But her story is just beginning.

''There's quite a few things that happened to me, to my daughter.

''We'd moved to Vicksburg after Elvis's first concert. Now in 1979 we had an incident with our dog. We had a big police dog that bit someone that went past the house. And when the police officer came out, there in the backseat of the police car was Elvis Presley. I thought, 'Nah, this can't be him. He's supposed to be dead.' And I just shrugged it off and I never said anything. I told my husband, I said, 'You know what? There's this guy that was in the back of the police car and he sure looked a heck of a lot like Elvis.' But he looked ill, or maybe he wasn't feeling well or something.''

Of all the things that happened to Louise Welling, perhaps the strangest is this incident that involved her daughter.

''In the early 1980s my daughter Linda had an apartment. She had just moved in and she got home early in the morning and the maintenance man was already in the apartment doing some repair work. Linda thought she was supposed to let him in, and she asked him how he got in. The maintenance man told Linda, 'Well, your boyfriend let me in.' This kind of puzzled Linda, and she said, 'Well what did he look like?'

''And the maintenance man told her he was tall with dark hair and wearing western clothes. That didn't match the description of who she was seeing, so this kind of puzzled her. A couple of days later she gets this two page letter on her car and I wish that we had kept it. It could have been proof positive that Elvis was in Kalamazoo. I'm trying to remember the whole letter. It said a lot of things that he was going to do. It wasn't your usual letter of a guy wanting to know her. It said, 'My dearest Linda, you're a beautiful young lady.' He talked about leaving in a week to go to Europe, and when he got back maybe they could get together for coffee. Someday she was going to be his 'little princess.' And it was signed 'EP,' just with the initials 'EP.' It had only happened the one time."

There was a further mysterious communication with Linda Welling.

"Linda had moved back home, and about 1983 she was in the hospital. Someone called the hospital and said they were Elvis Presley and to give Linda the best of care, and so on and so forth. And there wasn't anybody that we knew that would've played a joke. So we don't think it was a joke, we really think it was the real thing. No one has ever come forth and said we did this joke on you.

"He *was* here. He had connections."

One of Louise's big regrets is throwing out the letter her daughter had received.

"I know if I'd kept the letter . . ." Her voice trails off in regret, but she is not ashamed to admit it was her fault.

"I'm the dummy that threw it away. Being a mother, I thought, oh God, it's some kook. At that time I hadn't put it all together.

"See, I had the clue in my hand and I threw the darn thing away. I could kick myself every time I think about it."

Her most famous encounter with Elvis came in a widely reported sighting in a Vicksburg grocery story. It was covered in dozens, if not hundreds, of newspaper across the country. It also led to a short-lived Elvis frenzy in Kalamazoo, where storekeepers filled their windows with signs that carried slogans such as, "Elvis worked here" or "Elvis rents his movies here." Despite the lighthearted way her story was taken, Mrs. Welling has no doubts about what she saw that day.

"I saw him in the grocery store this one Sunday in 1987. I remember that really well. We had gone to church and every Sunday I stop at the store for something or other. I thought it was really odd this one particular Sunday because no one was in there, not even a customer, or so I thought. Not even the girls at the checkout.

"Then I went and got my things, and when I walked up to the counter there he was. I really believe I looked at Elvis Presley, just like I saw him in the police car."

She is commonly asked why she didn't do anything or say anything to Elvis. Her answer is simple and very human.

"I was kind of stunned. Everybody says, 'Well why didn't you talk to him?' and I think because I'm not that kind of a person that will just jump on someone and say 'Hey!' It kind of stunned me for a little bit, and I just kept looking at him, and I didn't believe it. I couldn't get anything out.

"He just smiled at my grandson who was with me. Whatever he got, it sure wasn't groceries because I couldn't see anything big on the counter. Whatever it was, it must have been tiny. I thought it was a fuse or something. He didn't have a big bag of groceries or anything when he went out.

"I really feel that from time to time he does come here. He had a connection to that hotel."

Welling was asked why she thinks Elvis has remained hidden for so many years. She disagrees with a popular theory.

"Some people say he was doing undercover work for the government and this and that, but I don't know. I really don't know. I sometimes wonder."

While discounting the idea that Presley was involved in some kind of secret operation, Welling has her own, much simpler idea. It must be said that her opinion, while not as exciting as the undercover hypothesis, is more believable and more in keeping with human nature.

"Maybe he just plain wanted to rest and get out of it. And people make me laugh, they say, 'Why would Elvis do this?' Well why wouldn't he? If you were as popular as he was, and you had all these girls screaming and hammering at you every minute, you'd want to run and hide. I don't understand why people don't think he'd do that. He'd be my number one choice for doing it."

Welling also has her own ideas about the periodic rumors that Elvis is about to make himself known publicly.

"I've heard about it for so long I've kind of given up. I hope I'm around to see it if it does happen."

And there is one aspect to the story that upsets Louise Welling.

"You know what the darndest thing is that makes me really, really angry is Priscilla Presley. She's not telling the truth. There's so much to Kalamazoo; I know she's got an aunt that lives here."

Another little known piece of the Elvis puzzle occurred shortly after Elvis's supposed death. Louise provides us with the fascinating details.

"This is another thing that happened. This is really important. About a week after Elvis's funeral there was a man here in Kalamazoo who came on our TV station and said he saw Elvis walking up Millham Road to Oakland Drive. And they interviewed him. And when all this Elvis stuff was going on, and I saw him in the store, they were all poking fun at me. Why didn't they return to this man? They never did.

"I tried to talk to one of the ladies that I knew who interviewed him. There were two ladies. Well one of them who moved to Grand Rapids, she got scared as a chicken and told me she never worked for Channel 3. I know that was an out-and-out lie. I really feel that she is covering something up. I believe this with all my heart.

"The other lady is kind of a snotty lady and she won't talk to me. So why won't she talk to me? If there's nothing there, she could at least talk to me, prove me wrong or something. But I know that happened. In fact, there's a man that works for the convention bureau here in Kalamazoo who had told me that some lady in the Burger King was telling him that that happened here too. But I already knew that had happened."

In the end, Louise Welling remains convinced that Kalamazoo is a likely place for Elvis Presley to be seen.

"See there's more to Kalamazoo than people know. They can poke fun, but there's a lot they don't know."

It's true that press accounts rarely mention the facts Louise Welling has accumulated about the Kalamazoo area. Most stories that appeared in 1988 tell Louise's story in a paragraph or two, simply saying that she saw Elvis in the grocery store. In almost no instance are the important details about Elvis's connections to the area given any play.

Frequently, Louise is made fun of, especially by columnists. She doesn't care about this. She'll just tell the truth as she knows it.

"I don't care what they say. The more you tell the truth, the harder you tell the truth, it's got to pull through one of these days. It has to. I just know it. I'm not giving up."

Nor is money her motive.

"I'm not making it up. I never have. I'm not gaining anything. I'm not making any money or anything."

Someday, perhaps, the whole truth will be revealed. Louise Welling is waiting for that day. If it happens, she will have been a big part of it.

"I figure one of these days it will happen. I guess God's just waiting for the right time, or for all of them to hang themselves.

"But it has to pull through some day."

MORE FROM
KALAMAZOO

Not long after the first sightings of Elvis in Kalamazoo, Kelly B. decided to investigate. The sightings had intrigued her, and she wanted to know more. She wasn't one to wait around for answers. She decided to find them herself.

She needed some kind of clue. After asking around, she got the tip she needed. She learned that there was a mysterious owner of an office building in town. The man's name was "John Burrows." Kelly had heard that John Burrows was an alias that Elvis Presley often used. She also heard that this John Burrows was said to resemble Elvis. This was all the information she needed. She would check it out herself.

She arrived at the building and went directly to work, entering offices and asking the people there if they had seen Elvis Presley or John Burrows.

"They all looked at me quite incredibly," she said. "I mean, these are business people and I'm asking them for Elvis Presley."

Kelly wasn't going to let strange looks intimidate her.

She continued to go from office to office, searching the building. Finally, a security guard stopped her. He asked her to come into an office with him.

To her great surprise, when Kelly walked in, there was Elvis Presley.

"I turned around and looked directly into his eyes," she said. "He had on gold rim glasses, a very modified version of what he used to wear, with a slight tint to them."

It wasn't the glasses that convinced her, however, it was the eyes of the King.

"I looked into his eyes. He had the Elvis Presley expression in his eyes, which I think most people that know him are familiar with."

It was a special look that Kelly insists could belong only to one man.

"The eyes had that kind of sparkle. They were the same shape and the same color eyes as Elvis had."

She confronted him with her belief. "I was stunned. I said, 'You have eyes just like Elvis. Are you related to him?' He said, 'Nope.' "

She spoke to him briefly. "Then after he listened to my questions, he just stood there with a very pleasant look on his face, kind of half smiling at times. And just before I walked away he said, 'Yeah, but it's against the law to hoax your death.' "

That was all Kelly saw of him. She never saw Elvis again, because Kelly died not long after her meeting with him. But she remained convinced that she had seen Elvis Presley.

DOING THE WASH

East Lansing, Michigan.

Marty P. was heading to the laundromat with a load of clothes and a fistful of quarters. It was about seven o'clock on a Thursday evening. He'd just finished dinner and needed to get some clothes washed so he'd have something to wear that weekend. He was going to a local club to see a heavy metal group, which was the only kind of music he listened to.

He got to the laundromat and, as he always did, took the machine in the far back of the store. He liked that one because the back door opened onto an alley and a little air would come in and help cool the overheated laundromat. He was reading a music magazine, waiting for his clothes.

Marty sensed some movement in the corner of his eye and looked up. Strangely, someone was coming in the back door. He'd been here a hundred times and no one had ever entered that way. It was a large man, wearing dark glasses, blue jeans, and a white cowboy shirt. He had a small bundle of clothes with him.

"Excuse me," he said to Marty, "is this machine

taken?'' He pointed to the washer next to the one Marty was using.

''No,'' Marty replied, thinking nothing of it.

''Sorry to bother you,'' the man said, ''but I haven't got any change. Could you break a dollar or two for me?''

Marty had plenty of quarters, but he also knew there was a change machine at the front of the laundromat. He told the man about it.

''That's fine, fine,'' the man replied. ''But you see . . .''

He seemed to be stumbling a little, searching for words.

''It's the light,'' he said. ''My eyes are very sensitive to light, and I'd rather not go to the front by that big plate glass window. I'm sorry if it's any trouble . . .''

''No trouble,'' Marty said. ''I can spare a dollar or two.''

It seemed rather strange to him, this whole exchange, but he figured the guy was a little weird. That didn't bother Marty. Most of his friends were a little weird too. In fact, Marty considered himself a bit weird, in a cool, heavy metal way, and he figured if the guy doesn't want to use the change machine, what do I care? After all, people usually gave Marty strange looks as he sat alone way in the back of the laundromat.

Bored with waiting, Marty thought he'd talk to the guy. He made a few commonplace remarks, just some obvious icebreakers, things like, ''Sure is hot in here, huh?'' But the big man wouldn't take the bait. He'd nod politely, say ''Sure is'' or ''Seems that way,'' but wouldn't enter into any further conversation.

Marty figured he didn't want to be bothered, so he gave up trying. Still, there was something familiar about him.

Finally, the man's laundry was done. He picked up his bundle, turned to Marty and said, ''Thanks again for the change.'' He started to walk out the back door, when suddenly he turned around. Pointing at the magazine lying on the chair next to Marty, the magazine with a long-haired heavy metal band on the cover, the man said, ''You know, you might want to try listening to some other kind of music sometime. Give this a try.'' He reached into his back pocket and flipped Marty a cassette tape. ''Thanks again,'' he said, and he stepped quickly out the back door, down the steps into the alley.

Marty stood there a second. Then he looked at the cassette. The title hit Marty like a lightning bolt. *Elvis In Person.*

''Oh, my God,'' he said to himself. *''That's* who he looked like!''

Marty jumped out the door and cried out, ''Hey fella, wait a minute!'' But he was too late.

He turned his head just in time to see a large white car turning out of the alley.

Weird, Marty thought. Then he felt some doubts. *No, it couldn't have been him. It was just some guy with bad eyes who didn't want to go to the front of the laundromat.*

Then something else occurred to Marty. Bad eyes. He didn't like the sunlight. Marty looked up. The sky was nothing but clouds. There had been no light coming through that plate glass window. It was just an excuse to stay in the back of the laundromat.

Marty looked at the tape again. *Elvis in Person.*

''Nobody's gonna believe this,'' he said.

He sat down and waited for his laundry, just watching it spinning around, wondering about what had happened.

When he got home, he sat down and put the tape on the stereo. He stared out the window at the clouds, listening to the music. *This stuff's pretty good,* he thought. *Maybe I ought to listen to it a little more often.*

JUST MISSED HIM!

Syracuse, New York.

"Treat Me Nice" was playing on the cassette deck when Hank R. went in to shave. He started every morning with Elvis. Hank loved the King. He had dozens of albums, watched his films every time they came around on television, and covered his walls with Elvis photos and posters.

It wasn't a lot of wall space to cover. Just a trailer in a trailer park on the outskirts of Syracuse, New York.

Hank was a hardworking, meat and potatoes guy. He worked on a road repair crew during the day and spent most of his nights in his favorite bar shooting pool, hanging out with the boys, sometimes putting the moves on a lady. It was a simple life, but all he ever wanted.

Hank was basically content but for three main complaints in his life. First, there were never enough Elvis songs in the jukebox at the bar. No matter how often Tommy, the owner, would increase the number of Elvis songs, Hank was never satisfied. There were probably fifteen Elvis songs in the old jukebox, but Hank always bugged Tommy for more. Every couple of months Tommy

29

would add a new one to keep him happy. After all, he didn't want to lose one of his best customers.

His second main complaint was his car. It was a classic 1960 Chevy he'd come across and bought on the cheap. It took a few years of working on it in his spare time, but he had it looking like new. Hank added a modern car stereo so he could play his Elvis tapes, but everything else in the car was vintage.

He would tell people that he never got married because he was already married to his car. "Wouldn't be fair to marry a woman," he'd say, "because I've already got a date every weekend."

The only reason the Chevy was his second main complaint in life was because of the trouble Hank had getting parts when something broke. His friends said that every other time you'd ask Hank, "How's it going?" you would get a story about him tracking down hard-to-find car parts.

His third complaint was more serious. It was Elvis's death.

The whole thing struck him as peculiar right from the start. When he heard the news he was heart-stricken, like so many of the King's fans. But when he started thinking about it, the whole thing didn't seem right.

A heart attack? That was the story. *Sure, Elvis had gotten overweight,* Hank thought, *but he had too much life to go that way.* He'd believe it of almost anyone else, but he couldn't believe the King would go down like that.

Hank carried his doubts with him for years. Sometimes he'd mention them to friends. They'd always call him crazy. But Hank knew all along that something was funny.

Trouble was, he had no way of knowing what. He had no access to information, no way of learning the truth. He used to talk about going down to Memphis to find out for himself, but he never really believed he would. He was so angry about the whole thing.

Then one day, he came across a small item in the newspaper.

There was a new book out claiming Elvis might never have died. That was it! He didn't have to read the book to know it was true. He kept that clipping and carried it in his wallet. He started telling everyone down at the bar that Elvis lived. Some of them had heard the stories, but they still thought it was all a hoax. Hank even got into fights over it. Pretty soon, all the regulars down at the bar avoided him any time he was busy "talkin' Elvis," which is what they called it.

"Oh boy, Hank's talkin' Elvis again!" The call would go up and they'd all walk away from him. Mostly, he took it with a smile and dropped the subject.

Hank still started his mornings with Elvis. This morning was like every other. Get up, shave, get off to work, pick up some quick breakfast on the way.

It was overcast this morning. Hank hoped it wouldn't rain. Hank loved working out-of-doors, but a rainy day was just a pain he'd rather do without.

He was standing naked by the sink, lathering up his beard, when he saw some movement out of the corner of his eye. Someone had walked past his bathroom window. This was strange, because the bathroom window opened up on the back of the trailer, and he almost never saw anyone walking by first thing in the morning.

Hank moved over to the window and looked around. The window was small and he couldn't see very much, but he did see a man walking away. He only glimpsed him from the back, but he never had a moment's doubt. It was the King.

What should he do now? He ran into his bedroom and grabbed his pants. He started running to the door while trying to pull his pants on, but he got tangled and tripped, crashing into the kitchen table. His head took a hard knock, and a glass fell to the floor and shattered, scattering shards everywhere. Hank staggered to his feet, yanked up his pants, and proceeded to step right onto a big, jagged piece of broken glass. It cut into the soft underside of his bare left foot. Hank screamed in pain. He grabbed the foot and yanked the glass out. He was bleeding all over the floor, but that wasn't going to stop him. He kept heading for the door.

He flung the door open and started out. In his haste, he stumbled again, tumbling down the short flight of stairs leading up to his trailer. He took the fall hard. His right elbow got the brunt of it, and his arm felt numb from the shock. But the King was somewhere around and Hank would have run through machine-gun fire to get to him.

He ran around to the back of the trailer as fast as his bleeding foot could go. The loose gravel and small, sharp rocks all around weren't making it any easier. When he got there, he stopped dead. No one was there.

"Oh shit!" he muttered. "Where in hell is he?"

"It must've been quite a sight," Hank said later, remembering standing there in the cold with no shirt or shoes, his bleeding left foot held in his hand, his right elbow scraped and bruised, and a face full of shaving cream! And all for nothing!

There was no sign of Elvis anywhere. He looked for a car, but nothing was moving along the road. Dejected, Hank hopped back to his trailer. All he had to show for it was a cut foot, a bruised elbow, a broken glass, and a trail of bloody footprints from his kitchen to his door.

He called in sick to work that day. He had to get the foot stitched, and the elbow hurt him for weeks. When people asked him about it he more or less told the truth.

"I broke a glass in the morning and I stepped right on a piece."

And the elbow?

"I slipped coming down the front stairs."

It wasn't lying. It was just leaving a few details unsaid.

It took him a while to tell anyone the rest of the story, but Hank's tale became a legend down at the bar. He admitted to it late one night, telling two friends whom he swore to secrecy. But this was too good to hold in, and they spread the story the first chance they had.

As usual, Hank took it in a good-natured way. Tommy, the owner, was so impressed he ordered five more Elvis songs for the jukebox. Every few months some newcomer to the bar will hear about the story. He'll go ask Hank and Hank will be happy to tell it—as long as you buy him a beer.

But how could Hank be so sure it was Elvis? After all, he just glimpsed the man from the back. Couldn't it be anyone with a similar build and hairstyle?

He tells it in his own words:

"Sometimes you just know something. If it were most other people telling this story, I'd say they was crazy too. How could anyone tell it was Elvis seein' him so quick? It's a good question.

"But other people ain't me. I know Elvis. Truth is I had a feeling even before I looked out that window. I seen enough for me. You don't have to believe me. I don't expect you to. But now I know for myself that he's alive. And that's good enough for me."

But why would he be in a trailer park in Syracuse, so far from his usual haunts?

"Well how should I answer that? I can't be expected to understand the actions of a man like Elvis. Why is he in hiding? Who knows the reason? Whatever it was, he had a reason for being there. Because he *was* there. And I got the scar on my foot to prove it!"

ELVIS WHO?

Elvis Presley meant nothing to Myrna W. Not even when he spoke to her.

Myrna was a craftsperson. She lived in a rural area of upstate New York and made wreaths that she sold at craft fairs. They were lovely creations, most of them with holiday themes. There were Christmas wreaths, full of holly and berries, Santas and reindeer, and lots of artificial snow. There were wreaths with turkeys and Pilgrims for Thanksgiving. Wreaths with bunnies and chicks for Easter. Heart-shaped wreaths for Valentine's Day. Anniversary wreaths. And her specialty was Halloween wreaths. They were charmingly creepy, covered in webs and spiders or small, withered witch-faces.

They were marvelous wreaths and Myrna sold a lot of them, but she didn't do it for a living. She had a good deal of money from her days as an art dealer in New York City. For thirty years she and her husband had run one of the richest art galleries in the city. Nearly all the great artists from the 1940s to the 1960s had been through their hands at some point. Myrna's husband had a genius for spotting the next big thing long before anyone else did, and he always managed to buy a lot of work when the price was low. It didn't take long for them to become wealthy.

During that time they lived in a large apartment, one of those old, New York apartments with high ceilings, huge, beautiful rooms, and a graciousness that no amount of money can build anymore.

Wrapped up in her world of high art, Myrna mostly missed the rock and roll revolution. She vaguely heard of Elvis in the fifties and the Beatles in the sixties, but none of it stuck with her. Her taste in music was opera. She read only the classics. She rarely even saw any films. Popular culture was something that existed on the farthest periphery of her life. It never mattered to her. Art was her whole world.

When her husband died suddenly, the gallery no longer meant anything to her. The two of them were so deeply intertwined after all their years together that she couldn't face the gallery without him.

Two decades earlier they had purchased a lovely house far upstate, to which they went for a month in the summer and a month in the winter. The rest of the time it was tended by a caretaker, who had it ready for them each time they made the long drive to their getaway home. The day her husband died Myrna knew she would move there. She didn't mind being so far away from people. She would have her books, her opera recordings, and a choice selection of art. Besides, she felt she would die shortly after her husband. They had often talked about their deaths, and both felt they would die close together.

That was one of the few things they were wrong about. Myrna outlived her husband by over twenty years.

The first few years went by peacefully for Myrna. She just drifted along, keeping herself busy with the grounds, writing letters to friends, occasionally having guests visit, always expecting to die at any moment. But time went on and on, and Myrna did not die.

Eventually, Myrna felt something she had never felt before in her life: boredom. She needed a hobby, so she turned to making wreaths. With nothing but time on her hands and enormous patience, Myrna worked away at her new craft until she was satisfied enough to present her wares to the public. She signed on to a number of craft fairs that were held within driving distance of her house, and she looked forward to them each year.

It was at one of these in 1989 that Myrna ran into Elvis.

It was late in September at an outdoor fair. The sun was going down and most of the other people selling crafts had packed up and gone. There were just a few customers milling around. Myrna was usually the last one to leave because she had nowhere to go and was never in a hurry. She had started packing when two men came over to her table and began looking at her wreaths.

She thought nothing of it at first, but there was something admirable about one of the men. He had a striking presence. He was dressed casually, except for one very large gold ring, but he seemed somehow larger than life. Myrna even felt there was something familiar about him, but she couldn't place it. Something far away in her mind started to stir, but she couldn't bring it to consciousness.

The two men looked at the wreaths. The man with the golden ring selected several of the spookiest Halloween wreaths. He turned to the man with him and said, "Lisa will just love these."

Then he turned to Myrna and asked, "Did you make all these yourself, ma'am?"

Myrna said yes.

"That's quite a talent you've got there," he told her.

The man then paid for the wreaths and left. Myrna watched him go, still wondering about him. But it was getting dark, so she put it out of her mind and finished packing her things.

A few weeks later she was reading a news magazine. She very rarely did this, but some friends were visiting and they brought it with them. There was a short story about Elvis Presley in it, and there was a picture of him as well.

That was he, she said to herself, *the man with the golden ring.* It was enough to make her remember the years past when Elvis first appeared. She had heard of him then, though she had long since forgotten.

Myrna's friend Estelle walked into the room at that point, and Myrna said to her:

"You know a few weeks ago I sold four wreaths to Elvis Presley."

Estelle looked shocked.

"Elvis Presley? But he died ten years ago."

"No, he didn't," Myrna said. "I saw him a few weeks ago and he bought four Halloween wreaths. They were for someone named Lisa."

Estelle couldn't believe what she was hearing.

"Lisa is his daughter. But you must be mistaken, Myrna!"

"I don't think so," she said. "He looked just like this picture in this magazine, only a little older."

"But he's dead!" That was all Estelle could think to say.

Myrna still didn't believe it. Looking down at the magazine, she started to read the story, and sure enough it said that Elvis Presley had died in August of 1977.

"But how could that be?" Myra wondered aloud. "I'm sure it was he. I just know it was he. It couldn't have been anyone else."

Estelle had heard some of the stories of Elvis's being alive, but she had always considered them crazy. And she knew Myrna had no interest in Elvis Presley and would never make up something like this. Myrna couldn't possibly have been playing a joke on her, because Myrna never played jokes on anyone. As far as Estelle was concerned, Myrna must have seen him or someone who looked just like him. It was a mystery that would never be solved.

Myrna considered the whole affair to be a little strange, but she never gave it much thought afterward. If Elvis was alive or not was really no concern of hers. She hoped he was, because she didn't like to think of anyone's being dead. But that was as far as her concern went. She still listens to opera, and she still makes her wreaths. And if you ask her about the time she met Elvis Presley, she has to think about it for a minute before it all comes back to her.

"Elvis Presley," she'll say. "Yes, I met him. They say he's dead, but I'm not in the habit of selling wreaths to dead people. I really don't know anything about him, but as far as his being dead is concerned, I know what I saw, and it would seem to me that somebody is very much mistaken."

SINGING IT
ONE MORE TIME

Shreveport, Louisiana.

The night was hot and damp. Troy had finished up a long overtime shift at the service station, and he wanted to relax. Fixing cars was tiring work, and he was ready to have steak and a beer and listen to the band.

It was Thursday night, his favorite. This was sing-along night at the bar and grill, when people from the audience could get up on stage and sing along with the band. Some of his friends would be there, and they'd have fun laughing at the people who tried to sing. It was all in good fun, and most people laughed at themselves as well.

Troy would try it himself once in a while, but tonight he was too weary from putting in all those extra hours. Business was good lately, and he had a lot of money to show for it. He'd buy a round or two for his friends, he thought, as he stepped out of the damp night into the cool, air-conditioned bar.

The band was playing dance music when he entered. The sing-along hadn't begun. Troy saw a few of his friends and sat down with them. It sure felt good when he got that first beer. He'd been craving it for hours.

The sing-along began, and it was one of the best ever. There were the usual amateurs who could barely carry a tune. They tried, and the crowd applauded appreciatively at their efforts. But the big story tonight was a young woman named Ada. When she took the microphone, everyone expected the usual bad singing. She asked the band to play "Losing You," the old Roy Orbison song. It was a difficult song to sing, with high, drawn-out notes, and Troy prepared for the worst. The band began the tune, Ada stepped up to the mike, and what happened next was magic.

Her voice was beautiful. She carried the song perfectly, right on top of every note, infusing the words with feeling. Troy had never heard Roy Orbison's words sound so powerful before.

When the song ended the crowd erupted in wild applause. Everyone there felt that they had witnessed the birth of a star. Who was this woman? Why had they never heard this voice before?

Ada sang several more songs. It was a spellbinding night, each song a gem. Ada tried to stop but the crowd demanded one more song. She complied, but then refused to sing anything else. She was too tired, she said. She hadn't really prepared for tonight, and she didn't want to hurt her voice.

Nobody could argue with this, and the crowd ceased imploring her for more. It was the talk of the night. For hours, conversation turned again and again to Ada's singing. And somewhere in the midst of it all, Ada slipped out the door. Nobody knew who she was, and she never returned to the bar.

But this was just the beginning of the night's mystery.

Many hours later, most of the patrons had gone home. Troy lingered with a few of his friends. The band had just quit, and they started to pack up, when a stranger approached them. He had been sitting with two other people in the darkest corner of the bar. Nobody had paid him any mind all night. They were too transfixed by Ada's singing.

The stranger approached the band and asked them if they could play one or two more songs. The guitarist told him no, they were through for the night. Then the stranger made an offer.

"I'll give you five hundred dollars," he said. "For three songs."

None of the musicians believed him.

"I mean it," he said. "Here, take a look at it."

Sure enough, he handed over five one-hundred-dollar bills. This was an offer too good to refuse. The bar didn't pay them that much for the whole night's work, surely they would play three more songs for that kind of money, no matter how tired they were.

Troy had already stayed far later than he should have. He rose to go home for some much needed sleep, when one of his friends stopped him.

"Hold on, Troy," he said. "Take a look at this guy. He looks like Elvis Presley!"

Troy turned his tired eyes toward the band. It was true. The singing stranger did look a lot like Elvis Presley, only older than in pictures of him.

"It's just one of those Presley imitator guys," Troy said. "I've had enough tonight; I'm goin' home."

"No, wait a minute," his friend James said. "This could be funny; stick around."

Troy didn't really want to, but he never liked to walk out on a friend, so he sat down.

The stranger took the microphone, turned toward the crowd and said, "Good evening, ladies and gentlemen. My name's Elvis Presley."

The dozen or so people remaining just laughed.

"Sure ya are!" one man called out, "And I'm Buddy Holly!"

"Should I prove it to you?" the would-be Elvis said. "Why don't you make a request?"

"OK," the heckler called back. "Sing 'Jailhouse Rock.' "

"You got it," Elvis replied.

He turned and said a few words to the band, then he took a classic Elvis stance on stage.

The band was tired, but they felt obliged to do their best for the kind of money they had been given. Like a weary fighter who finds strength for one last attack, the band pulled itself together and launched into a fiery version of "Jailhouse Rock." They never expected the singer would be even hotter.

He tore into the famous opening words.

The spectators, most of whom were watching sleepily, felt like a thousand watts had jolted through their seats. They couldn't believe the voice they were hearing.

"Great God Almighty," Troy said. "This old boy sounds just like Elvis."

By the time he finished, the people were on their feet, stamping and cheering.

"How's that, Buddy Holly?" Elvis called to the heckler.

"I guess you are Elvis!" the man called back. "Now how about 'Burning Love'?"

" 'Burning Love'? Hey I'm gettin' kind of old here. You must be trying to wear me out."

The crowd urged him on, begging for the song.

"Well all right, all right," Elvis said. "If I'm not dead yet, one more song won't kill me."

With these words, something clicked in Troy's head. All this time he had believed he was watching a very good Elvis impersonator; maybe even a great Elvis impersonator. But it occurred to him now that this guy was too good, too close a copy. Nobody could look that much like Elvis and sound that much like Elvis and act that much like Elvis without *being* Elvis.

He turned to James.

"I think this guy's Elvis," he said.

"Of course he's Elvis," James laughed back. "Who the hell else would he be?"

"No, I don't mean he's acting like Elvis," Troy said, "I mean I think he really *is* Elvis. For real."

"Ain't nobody told you yet maybe, Troy, but Elvis is dead. He's been dead a long time now."

"I still say it's him," Troy replied, getting angry at his friend. *But why should he believe me,* Troy thought, *of course Elvis is dead. James is right. I must be crazy.*

Onstage, Elvis was burning up the room with his rendition of "Burning Love." It was hotter than his first number, and the people went crazy when he finished.

Elvis seemed drained by the two numbers. He was sweating and looking a little pale. When he asked for a drink nearly everybody in the bar offered to buy it for him, but the bartender said it was on the house. Elvis asked for a glass of water.

People were shouting out requests for more songs, while Elvis sat on a chair catching his breath.

Finally, he took up the microphone again.

"Thank you so much," he said, as the spectators spontaneously applauded again.

"It's great to hear applause like that," he said, "It's been a long time."

Troy's eyes widened at those words. *It* is *him,* he thought to himself. *It* is *Elvis, the* real *Elvis.*

Troy was convinced, but he wasn't going to say anything yet. He'd hold on for a while to see what else happened.

Elvis spoke again.

"I'm afraid I'm a little out of practice," he said. "My stamina's not too good, so I'll just do one more number for you."

Everyone begged and shouted for more.

"No, I'd better not," Elvis said. "It's late and I've got to get going. But I'll leave you with a special song.

"I know we all heard Ada singing earlier tonight, and I must say she was one of the finest singers I've ever heard. She sang a number of Roy Orbison songs. I'd like to finish with another song from Roy. He was an old friend of mine, and I hope that up there in heaven he doesn't mind that I've changed a few words in his song.

"It's a great old song called 'Running Scared.' Like I said, I've changed it a little. Not too much, but enough to make it mean a little more to me. Listen closely."

Troy was fully attuned to Elvis now. He had a feeling that this song would be the final piece of the puzzle, the proof he was looking for. He wasn't disappointed.

The song began. The drummer tapped out the march-style drumbeat and Elvis began to sing. Troy knew the song, and he knew the words that were changed. The original song was about two lovers, and the man was afraid that another man was going to take away his girl. But Elvis had transformed it into a song about himself, a man on the run, a man trying to remain out of view.

But what was he doing up on stage? Why would he be singing this song if he wanted to hide? The song went on. *It was a challenge*, Troy thought. *He's daring us to find him out. Maybe he really wants to be found. Maybe he's sending a message that we should confront him and force him into the open.*

Troy thought further. *No, it wasn't a challenge. It's more of a plea. Elvis isn't sure. He wants to come back, he wants to be in the open, but for some reason he can't be, for some reason he has to remain hidden.*

The song was building. It was one of those songs that slowly increases in pitch until it peaks right at the end. It was a short song too, and the end was near. Elvis was now every inch the King. He stood straight and regal. He looked ten feet tall, defiant and proud.

The last note was impossible, it rose so high. The pitch

was crazy, but Elvis coasted in on a tidal wave of sound. It was the greatest singing Troy had ever heard.

There were only a dozen people watching, but when the song ended it sounded like a packed arena. All of them cheered like they had never cheered in their lives, nobody more so than Troy. It was Troy who started the chant.

"Elvis, Elvis, Elvis . . ."

The crowd took it up enthusiastically. They roared out the name, over and over. The band joined in, the drummer pounding out a beat. The building shook.

Over and over, Elvis thanked them. He seemed deeply moved by the applause and the shouting. Then one of the men who had been sitting in the corner with him came over and whispered something in his ear. Elvis nodded, and then picked up the mike for the last time.

"Thank you, thank so much," he said. "But I've really got to go now. I can't tell you how much this means to me, how good it makes me feel. I just wish I could do it more often."

With that, he put the microphone down, joined the two other men, and quickly headed out the door, people cheering him all the way.

Nobody thought to follow him, or ask him anything. He left as unexpectedly as he had appeared. It was all over.

Troy was certain now. There is no other singer in the world who could have done what he had just seen. Nobody. It was Elvis, the greatest, the King. Even after so many years, the voice was still the best.

But Troy didn't speak his thoughts to James this time, or to anyone else. He kept the knowledge to himself. He had to think it through.

It took him a while to reach a conclusion, but he did come to believe several things.

First of all, he has no doubt whatsoever that it was Elvis. Nothing in his life has been more certain than that.

Second, he feels pretty certain that Elvis wants to be left alone, or more likely has to be, for some reason. That night in the bar was just a moment Elvis couldn't pass by. It had been so long since he was in front of a crowd, singing his wonderful songs, that maybe he couldn't resist the temptation. The opportunity was there, for one night, and he took it. *It must have felt good to him,* Troy thought.

And finally, Troy was not going to spread the story. He'd admit to it if asked, and he'd tell the story if you wanted to hear it. But he wasn't going to go out of his way to publicize it. He'd rather keep it quiet, because he thinks that's what Elvis would want. And it was too late for the rest of the world because that night is gone and nothing can bring it back. Only a few people were privileged to hear Elvis, and most of them probably never knew whom they were hearing.

Troy believes that someday the King will return openly, that he'll come out of hiding to tell the world his story. But for now, Troy is happy to know that Elvis is still alive, and that he's still the greatest singer in the world.

For now, that will do. The rest of us will just have to wait for the day when Elvis can stop running scared and return to us all.

ASKING WHY

It is impossible to say just why Elvis Presley may have faked his death and gone into hiding, but speculation is possible, and there is some interesting evidence.

As with the theories of how he faked his death, there are two theories of why he did it. The first, and perhaps less interesting of the two, is that he faked his death to escape his own notoriety.

No evidence exists for this theory, but it accords well with human nature. Who wouldn't want to escape from the kind of life Elvis led, at least for a while? Imagine never being able to go anywhere without being mobbed, never being able to do the simplest things that most of us take for granted: walking down the street, going to a restaurant, shopping with his child. Of course, all celebrities have to face this to a certain extent, but there has never been anyone quite like Elvis, never anyone whose fans were so many and so enthusiastic. Normal life was so far out of his reach that when he wanted to take his daughter, Lisa, to an amusement park, he had to rent the entire facility for a day and allow only invited guests to enter.

This kind of existence must have been particularly tough on Elvis Presley, because unlike many celebrities, who enjoy their life of exclusive pleasures with the jet set, Elvis always remained true to his roots. He may have been rich and famous, but he was always a simple Southern boy at heart. He loved the common people, and no doubt he longed to be able to live among them at times, to enjoy the common pleasures of a picnic in the park or going to a baseball game with friends.

So it seems plausible that this may have been his motivation. Surely, we could understand his wanting to live a normal life. But this is also where this theory runs into some trouble. Just how normal a life could he lead, even after faking his death? If the numerous Elvis sightings that have occurred are any indication, Elvis cannot live in total freedom. People have recognized him again and again.

Yet even with that, his ability to move about must be greater now than it was before. As many of our stories attest, Elvis is frequently not recognized, at least not right away. Maybe some freedom is better than none at all.

The other theory of why he faked his death is both more extreme and, in some ways, more credible because there is some evidence for it. This theory contends that Elvis was working in some capacity as an undercover agent for the federal government, probably as a narcotics agent.

Elvis's concerns about the growing drug problem in America were well-known during his supposed lifetime. In fact, in 1970 Elvis met with then President Richard Nixon after writing to him and requesting a federal narcotics badge. Their meeting was not at all secret, and there is a famous photo of the two of them shaking hands. Yet what happened after that may have been quite secret indeed.

Elvis did receive the narcotics badge from President Nixon, and he was given credentials as a "Special Assistant" to the Bureau of Narcotics. It was Elvis's belief that he would function best as an "agent at large," not someone working full-time, but someone capable of getting close to underworld figures who wouldn't suspect him to be part of the law enforcement field. It is no secret that the music industry, and the entertainment industry in general, attracts drug dealers. Entertainers have big money, and they often have expensive tastes. This was especially true in the 1970s when drugs were still seen by many as glamorous and exciting, rather than as the destructive, deadly poisons everyone now knows them to be. Without doubt, many illegal operators must have tried getting close to Elvis, to tap into some of his wealth. Who better to be an undercover agent? Who better to learn the names of the big-time drug kingpins? That may be precisely what happened.

It is reported by many people that toward the end of his "life" Elvis was constantly in the company of serious-looking men in suits, men who had never before been part of his entourage. They were with him every day before the sixteenth of August in 1977. They were even reported backstage at his final concerts. Who were these mysterious men? It seems clear now that they were government agents.

Indeed, there is strong evidence to suggest that Elvis did precisely what he wanted to do as an agent-at-large: he fingered a very high-level drug dealer in Las Vegas. This led to contracts being taken out on his life and the lives of his family.

There is a further story that Elvis helped to indict a group of men who called themselves "The Fraternity." This was a loose-knit group of underworld figures who made money operating offshore banks used to launder illegal gains. It seems they were trying to get their hands on some of Elvis's money, though we are not sure quite how they tried to do this. Elvis, finding out about the scheme, notified the authorities. The men were eventually indicted for their illegal activities. But when they first learned of Elvis's involvement, there were threats made against his life, and several of his concerts were interrupted with bomb threats.

These are two instances that we know of. There may have been more. At any rate, it is clear that Elvis's life was at risk. This may have been the motivation to fake his death. He had to pretend to die so that he could continue to live.

It is possible that Elvis faked his death with the help of the government and its Witness Protection Program. Clearly, Elvis could not just "disappear" as an ordinary citizen might. He was far too famous for that. Some drastic step was needed. The only way to avoid questions and investigations of his whereabouts would be to pretend he had died.

It is also possible that Elvis's death was faked by a private group, not part of the government. This is speculative, but in Monte Nicholson's book *The Presley Arrangement,* he theorizes that there may indeed be private groups that will make a person "disappear" for a certain price. These are not necessarily illegal or underworld operations. In fact, the government may use such groups itself. The government often hires private sector businesses to do work. Usually, a private company can do the work faster, cheaper, and better than a government agency. Why should this not apply to the Witness Protection Program? Making people vanish from the face of the earth, creating new identities for them, cannot be an easy thing. Given the history of the government bureaucracy's bungling even the simplest of tasks, they could not be blamed for entrusting the disappearance of Elvis to a private group that could handle the case with efficiency and secrecy.

The undercover scenario may seem too much like a spy movie to be plausible, but as we have seen, there is evidence that points to just such a sequence of events taking place. It is not at all outside the realm of possibility. Indeed, it might be worth considering that both theories of why Elvis faked his death may work together. His life may have been threatened, and he may also have wanted to escape his fame. Faking his death would kill two birds with one stone.

HIDING IN
THE WILDERNESS

The Florida Everglades.

Joyce hiked into the Everglades every summer. It was the most important and the best part of her job. She was a prominent ornithologist at a major Florida university (she has since taken a job in a different state), and each summer she spent several weeks hiking into the wilderness to study the birds.

Her goal was to estimate populations. She visited known breeding areas to see if the bird populations were remaining stable. If there seemed to be a decline in a particular species, she would try to determine why. Several times she had discovered environmental damage, usually caused by illegal dumpers or careless people who shouldn't have been there. When she found a problem like that, Joyce would turn detective. Three times over the years she had tracked down the culprits and brought them to justice, but more often than not that didn't happen. It was too difficult to trace the source of the damage most of the time.

What she really enjoyed was the solitude. Many people might be afraid of traveling alone as Joyce did, and her

colleagues tried to persuade her not to do it. She knew
that the first rule of traveling into a wilderness area is
never to go alone. Anything could happen accidentally. A
twisted ankle, a snake bite, a broken leg: a hundred things
could go wrong, and if there was no one along to help
you, chances are you would die long before rescuers
reached you. Joyce knew all that, but she took her chances
because she liked nothing better than to be alone with
nature. Her one concession to safety was a CB radio she
carried. Twice a day she checked in with a colleague to
tell him she was safe.

It was on the third day of a planned five-day journey
that Joyce came across the strangest thing she had ever
encountered. Every year she made the same trip. She was
a skilled tracker and by using her compass she could travel
an almost identical route every year. That's why it was so
shocking to see a small cabin where there had never been
one before.

What was a cabin doing in the middle of the Everglades?
First of all, it had no right being there in a national park.
She had not heard of any park service plans to build such
a cabin, and she knew all the scientific studies going on,
and none of them included this. It must be some illegal
activity.

Several ideas crossed her mind. Perhaps it was a poach-
er's cabin, for someone trying to trap rare wildlife for sale
to underground markets. There was a large volume of trade
in illegal wildlife, but almost all the animals came from
less-developed parts of the world. She didn't expect anyone to be so brazen as to do it in the middle of Florida.

That idea seemed too farfetched, but her next idea
seemed more on target, and it made her nervous. She
thought it must have something to do with drug dealing.
Tons of illegal drugs entered the United States through
Florida, and perhaps the cabin functioned as some kind
of drop-off point, or a hideout for smugglers. This was
one time she wished she had a gun with her. She was a

crack shot with a rifle but normally didn't bring one with her. There was never a need for it, and it just weighed her down.

Her problem now was what to do. She didn't think she had been seen, so she ducked into the dense underbrush and watched the cabin closely. It was a small cabin that seemed to have just one room. There was a window on the side facing her, but the reflection on the glass prevented her from seeing anything inside. After observing the scene for over half an hour, she decided that the cabin must be empty at the moment. She understood the danger, but she felt she had to investigate.

She put down her gear and walked over quietly. Her years of experience tracking wildlife enabled her to move with the silence of a forest animal. No one inside would hear her approaching. When she reached the building she squatted beside it and put her ear to the wall, trying to hear if anyone was inside. She listened for several minutes, but heard nothing. Finally, she made her most daring move and looked into the window. For a few heart-stopping seconds she was terrified at her own bravery—or was it foolhardiness?—but she quickly saw that the cabin was empty, and she let out a great sigh of relief.

There was only one thing left to do. She had to go inside. This would leave her vulnerable if anyone came along, but she needed to find any evidence she could.

She walked slowly around to the door after carefully looking and listening for any movement in the area. When she tried the door she discovered to her surprise that it opened. She stepped in and closed it quietly behind her.

Wasting no time, she took a visual inventory of the room. There was very little to see. There were a few chairs, a small couch, a little bookshelf, and a table. There was also a small metal cabinet. She looked at the bookshelf first. It contained some writing paper and a box of pens and pencils. There were a few dozen books. Some were adventure novels, mostly westerns. A few more were religious books and books of a mystical nature. And a few more were books about Elvis Presley. It didn't seem like the bookshelf of a drug dealer, though she wouldn't know what a drug dealer's bookshelf *would* have.

Then she opened the metal cabinet. It contained an assortment of canned foods and some freeze-dried food. There were also some matches and some toilet items. Off in a corner were about twenty jugs of sealed springwater. And last of all, there was a guitar hanging on the wall with a crucifix close by. None of this added up.

Joyce didn't feel as nervous now, though she had learned nothing significant about the occupant. But it didn't seem like anything illegal was going on. If it were used for illegal purposes, she would expect to see some kind of communication equipment or some weapons, but there were no signs of either.

Not knowing what else to do, she left the cabin and continued on her way. She would certainly report it when she got back. Whatever the case, the cabin itself should not be there, and she wasn't going to allow whoever put it there to damage her beloved wilderness. But she had traveled three days already and didn't want to return now. It seemed like matters could wait, so she journeyed on. She would check it again on the way back.

It was about 9:00 A.M. on the last day of her trip, and Joyce was hiking back out of the Everglades. It was a long trip, but she didn't need to observe birds on the way out. She did have one stop to make, however, and that was at the cabin.

As she drew near to the area, she adopted her best hunting walk: crouching, silent as the breeze, she approached the cabin. Suddenly, she stopped dead. A voice. She could hear a voice. All her fear returned, but burning curiosity and blood-red anger made her continue. She dropped her gear so she could be as swift and silent as possible. She drew nearer and nearer, carefully darting from cover to cover to remain concealed. Joyce could sneak up on a sharp-eared deer, so she knew no one would spot her.

At last she drew close enough to hear clearly, but she still couldn't see anyone. The angle was wrong. She had to work her way around to the back of the cabin. It was a little risky, but she managed. The strange thing was she only heard one voice. It seemed to be someone talking to himself. The remarks she picked up were meaningless. Someone was cooking breakfast over a small gas grill, talking to himself about fixing the eggs and bacon. She could only see him from the back. She watched for twenty minutes while the man cooked and ate his food. All the while Joyce was torn by two impulses. Should she just walk out and confront this intruder into her wilderness, or should she sneak away and return with the authorities? Her good sense told her to go. Her anger made her want to confront him.

She was nervous, but there seemed to be nothing threatening about this man. Better safe than sorry, she finally decided, and she was about to make her way back to her gear when the man stood up. He stretched a bit, then walked a few feet over to where a guitar was standing against a tree. It must have been the guitar from the cabin. The man sat down on a large rock and began to strum the instrument. As he did so, he turned in Joyce's direction, and she was finally able to see his face.

She remembers the moment:

"Of course I didn't know what to expect, because I didn't expect anything. But when he turned around I gulped so hard I was sure he'd hear me. It was the image of Elvis Presley. It was crazy, but there he was as clear as could be. I had a perfect view of him.

"I wasn't prepared to believe it yet, however, but I certainly wasn't going to leave now. I'd stay there and watch as long as I could. Besides, he looked like he was about to sing. That would help me decide if it was really Elvis."

The song turned out to be the clincher. After a few

minutes of strumming and tuning the guitar, the man—
call him Elvis—began to sing.

"It wasn't any Elvis Presley song that I recognized, but
it sounded like a country song. I learned months later,
completely by accident, that it was an old folk song from
the Civil War, a song called 'Rebel Soldier.' At the time,
I didn't know that, but I could hear the words and they
were perfect for Elvis."

> Oh Polly, oh Polly, it's for your sake alone.
> I've left my old father, my country, my home.
> I've left my old mother to weep and to mourn.
> I am a rebel soldier, and far from my home.

"I just stayed there, mesmerized," Joyce said. "I forgot that I was lying uncomfortably in a pile of underbrush,
sweating profusely. My discomfort just disappeared. His
voice was beautiful. It was the voice of Elvis Presley."

Joyce was deeply moved by the song. One verse in particular struck her.

> I'll build me a castle, on some green mountain high
> Where I can see Polly when she is passing by,
> Where I can see Polly and help her to mourn,
> I am a rebel soldier, and far from my home.

Joyce recalls her emotions:

"When he sang those lines, you could hear the tremor
in his throat. Even from a distance, I swore I could see
the tears well up in his eyes. He hesitated for a moment
when he sang the part about being far away from home.
The song just paused for a few seconds, as if the truth of
it all was too much for him. Then he continued on. It was
the most wistful, saddest song I'd ever heard. If someone
could've recorded it, it would sell a million copies in a
day. I've never heard anything so beautiful."

When the song was over, Elvis just sat for a few minutes, perhaps contemplating the words he had sung so movingly. Then he got up and went into the cabin.

Joyce was faced with a dilemma. There was no way she could decide what to do at that moment. The situation was too extreme. It required some thought. She decided to return home as scheduled, and once there she would decide what action to take.

She made it back to her truck as quickly as possible. On the drive home, Joyce remembered something.

"In all the excitement, I had forgotten that a group of students from the university were planning a field trip into this area in two weeks. I wasn't running the trip, but I had been invited. I hadn't decided yet whether I would go, but now I knew I had to do something. They would certainly see the cabin, and that might be the end for Elvis. After hearing him sing that way, I couldn't betray his solitude. He must've been in that cabin to find some peace. Maybe he thought he found a place away from the world, but he was mistaken. I decided to help him."

A week later she returned to the cabin. It was very early when she arrived, and no one was around. She moved quietly over to the cabin and slipped under the door a letter she had written. The letter was brief.

Dear Elvis,

Please don't be alarmed. I saw you outside your cabin a few days ago. You were singing and I knew you were terribly sad. I didn't come over to you, and I'm not going to disturb your solitude now. I am writing this to warn you. A group of students from [a major university] will be coming into this area next week. I will be with them myself, and I can assure you this cabin will be discovered. If you don't want to be found here, please leave as soon as possible. Perhaps you thought this area was safe, but more people travel through here than you realize. Someone may find you at any time.

I hope I have helped you. God bless you, and I hope you find the peace you seem to be searching for.

With love, your fan and friend,
Joyce C.

A week later, Joyce returned to that spot with the group of students. The cabin was gone.

One of the students walked over to the exact spot when he suddenly called out to the others.

"Look at this!" he cried.

They came over and saw an indented area of crushed plants, in a perfect rectangular shape. It was clear that something had been there recently. No one knew what to make of it. Some of the students excitedly suggested that a UFO had landed there. Only Joyce knew the truth.

As the others argued over what could have made the strange depression in the ground, Joyce just gazed around, remembering the song. Then her eyes alighted on something. It was the large rock Elvis had been sitting on when he sang.

Something made Joyce walk over to it. She just wanted to be at that spot. When she got there, she saw that some words had been scratched into the rock's surface. The marks were light and a bit faded, but they were clear enough to read:

"Thank you. Love EP."

Joyce slowly reached out to the words. She ran her trembling fingers over them one time. Then she rubbed them away, never to be seen again.

GETTING INTO TROUBLE

Atlanta, Georgia.

Gary S. and Susanah H. were a couple who shared everything, especially a zeal for radical politics and a wild, aggressive streak. They were graduate students at a famous California university, both majoring in government. Their future was all planned out. They would finish school, move to Washington, D.C., and become staff members for their favorite congressman. They already had the deal in the works through Gary's father's connections. He was a famous ACLU attorney with powerful Washington friends.

They were in Atlanta for a political gathering, and they were staying at one of the city's finest hotels. It was their first day there, and they were in the lobby reviewing some papers as they waited for their ride.

Susanah looked up from her reading and noticed a group of five men walking toward the elevator. They were all dressed in three-piece suits, and most of them sported heavy gold jewelry.

This was too much for Susanah. She nudged Gary and

said, "Look at these guys. What a bunch of hicks. Somebody should tell them it's not 1975 any more."

Gary looked at them and laughed. But then a light came on in his head.

"Doesn't the one in the middle there look a lot like Elvis Presley?" he said.

"Of course he does," Susanah replied. "All these guys want to look like Elvis Presley."

"No really," Gary insisted. "I mean he looks a *lot* like Elvis Presley. Oh shit, maybe we're having an Elvis sighting!"

Gary had read about Elvis sightings. He considered them ludicrous, the product of fevered imaginations. Not for one moment had he given them any credence. But here he was, having his own Elvis sighting. He wasn't sure how to react. He didn't want to be part of something he looked upon with such disdain, yet he couldn't help but wonder.

By this point, the men had reached the elevators and were waiting to go upstairs. Gary, always one to act on impulse, turned to Susanah and said, "Let's go check this out."

"Gimme a break," Susanah said. "It's just some cornball Elvis impersonator. What's to investigate?"

"Come on," Gary persisted. "Let's check it out! Maybe it's really him. Anyway, it'll be fun! Let's do it."

"Gary, we're waiting for our ride."

"So he'll wait for us. What do we care? We'll never have an opportunity like this again."

Susanah still hesitated. Gary knew the one sure way to get her going.

"Are you afraid to go check this out? You're just afraid."

"I am *not* afraid," Susanah said, instantly fuming. "I might be too embarrassed to do something so ridiculous, but I am *not* afraid!"

Gary knew he had her now. It always worked.

"Well then come on, before they get away!"

Getting into Trouble

It was too late. As Gary and Susanah rose from their seats, they saw the elevator closing. They hurried over.

"Let's see what floor it goes to," Gary said.

They watched the floor numbers lighting up one after another. Luck was with them because the five men were the only people on the elevator. That increased the odds of getting the right floor number.

The elevator stopped at the sixteenth floor.

"Let's go," Susanah said.

"No, wait," Gary replied. "That could be someone getting on. Let's watch a little longer."

Gary had pressed the elevator button in the lobby. He was happy when he saw the numbers start to descend. The elevator returned all the way to the lobby without stopping. They had their floor. Now they needed a plan.

"OK," Susanah said. "What now? So we know what floor they're on. How do we know what room?"

They stepped into the elevator and pushed the button for sixteen.

"It's easy," said Gary. "We just knock on every door until we find them."

"What if they don't want to open the door? Or don't let us in?"

"We'll give them a story. We'll pretend to be somebody we're not."

"Like who?"

"What about hotel security?"

"Oh yeah, wearing jeans and T-shirts? That will be convincing. Hotel security guards are always wearing dark glasses and polyester suits."

"OK, not security guards." Gary was thinking. The elevator reached sixteen and they got out. There was no one to be seen. The hall was quiet.

"All right," Gary continued, lowering his voice. "We'll be maintenance. Or inspectors. We'll say we have to check the bathroom because the room downstairs says there's water dripping from the ceiling."

"You're crazy," Susanah said. "What a stupid excuse."

"Yeah, stupid. But watch it work."

They began at one end of the hall. They knocked on the first several doors and received no answers. On the fifth try, a woman opened the door. There were two children running around in the room, making a mess. This couldn't be it, Gary thought, so he pretended to have the wrong room number. The very annoyed woman slammed the door shut.

Two more rooms didn't answer.

On the eighth try, a man in a suit answered the door. He didn't look like one of the men with Elvis, but they didn't take a chance. Gary presented himself as a maintenance inspector. The man looked at him doubtfully. He hesitated a moment, but then he let them in.

Gary tried to look confident as he headed for the bathroom, where he'd pretend to check the sink. But this room was designed in the opposite direction from Gary's room, so he opened a door and walked into a closet. The man in the room was now very suspicious. He walked quickly over to his briefcase on the bed. He opened it up and pulled out a pistol.

"What the hell is going on here?" he growled at them.

Gary and Susanah froze. It was like a scene in a Clint Eastwood movie. The man was cold as ice as he stared at them.

"If you two are trying to come in here to rip me off, you'd better think twice about it! I'll blow you both to pieces before you can get anywhere near my stuff."

Gary figured he had to play out the part.

"No, really, I'm here to look at the sink." He felt completely lame as he tried to pass himself off as an inspector. Susanah was hopelessly terrified.

"It's just that, well, I'm new here. We're not regular staff workers. They just hired us as extra help, and I'm not sure where the bathrooms all are."

Gary didn't think he was convincing at all. But the man with the gun played along.

"The bathroom's over there," he said, pointing with the gun. "Go check it out."

Gary and Susanah quickly went to the bathroom. Once there, Gary rattled around under the sink for a minute, then they came back out.

"Well, everything seems fine," Gary said. "Sorry to bother you."

They started for the door. Just as they were about the leave, the man with the gun called to them.

"Hold it a minute," he said.

Gary and Susanah thought they were dead.

"You two are full of shit, aren't you?" the man said. "Admit it."

"Well, yeah, we are." Gary couldn't keep up the role any longer. "But we weren't trying to rip you off. We're trying to play a joke on someone, but I guess we got the wrong room. Sorry about it. I guess we were pretty stupid."

The man put the gun away.

"I got a little advice for you," he said. "Stay away from practical jokes. You never know what could happen."

"Thanks," Gary said, and he shot out the door.

Out in the hall, Gary told Susanah he'd had enough. "The hell with Elvis," he said, "let's get out of here."

But now Susanah wanted to take the upper hand.

"What, are you getting scared? So we made a mistake. Next time, we won't go into a room unless we're sure. We'll just pretend it's the wrong room. There's only a few more to try."

Gary wouldn't let Susanah get the best of him. The truth was most likely that neither of them wanted to continue this game, but no one wanted to be the first to back down. Fortunately, their luck changed on the very next try.

They knocked on the door. A man in a suit answered. They knew right away it was one of the men with Elvis.

"What is it?" he said, looking surly and annoyed.

Gary gulped a little, but he went ahead.

"Uh, we're here from building maintenance. We have to check the bathroom sink because somebody in the room beneath you reported a drip on the ceiling."

"Why didn't anybody call the room?" the man said. Gary saw he was slick and wouldn't fall for his ruse.

"And you got any identification?" he said, glaring at them.

This question did Gary in. After the man with the gun, Gary wasn't going the tackle another guy with nerves like this. He was about to make an excuse and back out, when Susanah decided to create a little chaos.

She bolted past the man at the door and ran into the room. She saw the four other men sitting around the coffee table. When they saw her they all jumped up. Elvis was in the middle of them, and they leaped in front of him. But Susanah saw enough.

"It's Elvis, it's Elvis," she began to shout. "I know it is! Admit it! Admit it!"

The man from the door grabbed her from behind. Gary came rushing over.

"Let her go!" he cried. He tried hitting the man on the back, but his hand crumpled against the man's powerful muscles. It hurt Gary more than it hurt him.

Then Gary was grabbed.

Elvis and the other two men snatched up the bags that were on the floor and headed for the door.

Susanah was still screaming "Elvis!" and "Let me go!" along with numerous four-letter words. Gary was more passive.

He was dragged to the bathroom and tossed inside. Susanah soon followed. Somebody pulled the door shut and held it closed. Gary tried to open it, but his strength was no match for the man holding the door.

Susanah continued to scream. "Let us out! Let us out! Help! Police!"

Finally Gary turned on her.

"Will you just shut up!" he cried. "Haven't we done enough!"

Susanah was shocked.

Just then, the doorknob on the outside of the door popped off. The man holding the door shut had pulled too hard. He fell backward and tripped over a footstool. This gave Gary and Susanah a chance to escape.

They went running out into the hall. They ran toward the elevators. Once again, they were moments too late.

The doors were closing on Elvis and the other men. But just before they shut, Elvis cried out.

"Why don't you people just leave me alone!"

The door closed. He was gone.

The epilogue to this story is interesting. Gary and Susanah are no longer a couple. When he told her to shut up in the bathroom, he committed what was to Susanah an unforgivable act. It came between them again and again. She kept bringing it up every time they had an argument. A few months later it was all over.

That was several years ago. Susanah has since fulfilled her ambitions and is now a rising star among congressional staffers. Gary, on the other hand, turned away from politics. It is from him that we know this story, and he should have the last words.

"I don't know what it was," he says. "Ever since that day, everything is different."

"I think it was the sense of intrusion. First, the guy with the gun. I still have bad dreams about it. But more than that, it was Elvis in the elevator. He looked so sad when he told us to leave him alone. It's strange, but I never looked at it that way before.

"I had always been aggressive looking for information. In politics, you have to be. I just considered it part of the game. It never occurred to me that what was information gathering to me, was really a tremendous personal intrusion to someone else. I mean, I was trespassing on something that was none of my business, and I was doing it just because I felt I had the right to do it. I never considered that Elvis might have a right to be left alone.

"I think that whole new sense of things got me out of politics. Politics is nothing but intruding on people's lives, telling them what to do. Maybe it's just none of my damn business.

"I feel terrible about that day. I wish there was a way I could make it up to Elvis, but of course the best way to do that is to just leave him alone. To just let it be. I'm certainly not going to try to find him and apologize!

"I'm a different person because of that day. I think I'm a better person. I have Elvis to thank for that. I wish there was a way I could tell him."

Postscript: Gary now works in the public relations department of a computer-related corporation, somewhere in California.

SHORT SIGHTINGS

Not all the encounters with the King are close or verifiable. A great many of them are brief glimpses, a figure seen turning a corner, passing by in a car, buying a newspaper. This is only to be expected. Without question, Elvis seems to be constantly on the move. Here are several brief encounters with Elvis.

Fond du Lac, Wisconsin. Martha G. was out shopping for groceries. On the way to her car in the parking lot, she spotted a man who seemed to look like Elvis Presley. He was standing next to a large Cadillac with tinted glass, speaking to a man in a dark suit. Elvis was wearing a denim jacket and jeans, and dark glasses. Martha quickly put her groceries in her trunk, never taking her eyes off Elvis.

She began to walk slowly toward him. She was about twenty feet away when the other man saw her. He said something to Elvis and pointed at Martha. Elvis turned suddenly and, with a look of frustration, quickly got into the car. The other man entered after him.

Martha started to run toward the car, but it was parked close to the exit from the lot. It pulled out quickly and sped away, leaving Martha behind.

Martha has no doubts about whom she saw.

"I've been an Elvis Presley fan all my life. I've seen him on film dozens of times, and I've been to sixteen of his concerts. I still have all the ticket stubs. I know what he looks like. I've seen plenty of Elvis impersonators, and none of them ever came close to fooling me. I know whom I saw."

Mobile, Alabama. Toby W. and Sam P. were out late driving. They decided to stop off for some beers at a late night convenience store. Pulling into the lot, they saw a fancy black Lincoln parked right in front of the doors. The engine was running, but no one was in the driver's seat. The rear windows were tinted too darkly to see through.

As they got out of their car, Toby complained to Sam about how the Lincoln was blocking the entrance. Just then a man came out of the store carrying a large bag of goods he had purchased. The man went to the back door of the Lincoln, opened it up, and handed the bag inside. He then sat down in the driver's seat, and pulled out of the lot.

It was only a moment, but Toby and Sam both swear that when the back door was opened, they had a clear view of who was in the backseat. It was Elvis Presley.

Kettering, Ohio. Barbara S. was up early that morning. She had to drive 150 miles for a sales meeting, and she wanted to get started with plenty of time to spare.

As she drove through town, she decided to stop off for some coffee. She pulled up to a store and went inside. There was one other customer in the store. He was buying a newspaper. Barbara didn't pay much attention to him. She felt sleepy and had a lot on her mind.

But when the man buying the newspaper said "You're welcome" to the young clerk who thanked him for his purchase, his familiar-sounding voice made Barbara look up. He passed by so close to her that her eyes couldn't focus on him quickly enough. She turned to watch him go out the door. As he turned away from the door, she saw his profile through the front window. It was Elvis Presley.

For a few seconds Barbara couldn't move. Then she ran out the door to look again, but it was too late. All she saw was a car driving away.

She returned to the store to ask the clerk if she had noticed anything familiar about the man who bought the newspaper. Unfortunately, the girl was not very observant, and she said he looked like any other customer.

Barbara asked if she could exchange her own dollar for the dollar Elvis had given the girl. The clerk looked at her as if she were crazy, but she did what Barbara asked. Barbara took that dollar with her to her sales meeting. She thought it would bring her good luck.

She sold more that day than she ever had before. She still has the dollar.

Wanda L. had just finished a hard morning at work. She was a countergirl at a delicatessen in Augusta, Georgia. That day, a construction crew had begun working in the area, and there were dozens of extra customers for breakfast. The morning had been nonstop work: pouring cups of coffee, buttering toast, scrambling eggs, wrapping orders. By eleven o'clock she felt exhausted. She had been working since 6:30 that morning, and only now did she have time for a break.

She decided to go for a short walk and sit down on the benches in a small square not far from the deli. All she wanted to do was relax for a few minutes, close her eyes, and rest her feet.

Her fifteen-minute break passed far too quickly. She

didn't feel rested at all, but it was already time to go back. With a sigh, she got up and started trudging back to work.

There was a florist shop that she would pass on the way back. As she approached it, she saw a man coming out of the store with a large bunch of flowers in his hand. They looked like roses, red and white mixed.

Isn't that great, Wanda thought. *Some lucky girl is probably going to get those roses today.*

Because her attention was drawn to the flowers, she didn't notice the man right away. He stepped off the curb and walked toward a double-parked car. It was a large car with darkened windows.

Wanda was still looking at the flowers when the man turned his profile toward her as he got into the car. The man was Elvis Presley.

Before she could move, the car door shut and Elvis drove away.

Wanda insists it was he.

"I don't have any doubt about it. It was clearly Elvis Presley. There's nobody else who looks like that. It must've been him."

It occurred to Wanda to ask the florist about it. She was already a little late for work, but this was more important.

She went in and asked the florist if he had just sold a bunch of red and white roses. He said he had. Wanda then asked if he noticed anything about the man who bought them.

"No," he said. "Except I was a little annoyed that he paid with a hundred-dollar bill. Business has been slow today and I had trouble finding enough change. When he saw that, he asked me if there was any kind of senior citizens' home in the area. I said, 'Yes, there's one a few blocks away.' He told me to keep the extra money and to use it to send as many flowers as it would pay for over to the home.

" 'Who should I send them to?' I asked him. He said

to say they're from someone who appreciates all that the elderly have given to the country over their lives.

"I said, 'That's it?' He said 'That's it.' And then he left."

Then Wanda asked him if the man looked familiar to him. The florist said no.

"Didn't he look like Elvis Presley?" she asked.

"Who?" he said.

Wanda realized that the florist wasn't even sure who Elvis Presley was. He wasn't going to be any help in identifying him.

The story of the flowers convinced Wanda. She knew Elvis had always been known for his generous gestures. This was typical of him. Who else would do such a thing? And what are the chances that the person who did it would also look like Elvis Presley?

For Wanda, there's no doubt at all. It was Elvis.

TALKING TO THE KID

The kid lit the joint for no reason at all. He was just getting high, like he did almost every day.

He watched as the Mississippi rolled by. Not far away was the magnificent Gateway Arch of St. Louis, that monumental symbol of all life's possibilities, an invitation to explore and discover. Sitting nearly in the shadows of this monument to human achievement, the kid puffed away, trying to forget the things he couldn't even remember.

The river traveled on, heedless of him. He stared blankly at the brown water. *That's my life,* he thought, *that's my life.* He didn't even know what it meant, but it seemed to fit.

He kept brushing his hair out of his face. It was long and dirty blond, hanging straight down. He wore a black T-shirt decorated with the insignia of a heavy metal band. His jeans were torn in all the right places. He puffed again, holding the smoke down for a moment, then he let it out and watched it float aimlessly away. *That's my life too,* he thought, and he didn't know what that meant either.

He heard footsteps. A man was approaching. Should he

throw the joint into the river? Nah, why waste it. This wasn't a cop, and no cop was going to care about him anyway, since he wasn't making trouble. *They've got too many more important things to do,* he thought.

The man came closer and closer. He seemed to be heading right toward the kid. *Get a load of this guy,* the kid thought, sneering at the man's cowboy boots and decorative, Western shirt. This guy looks like some lame Elvis Presley rip-off.

The man came right up to him.

"Can I talk to you a minute, son?"

He even sounded like Elvis, the kid thought. What the hell, he'd call him Elvis.

"Sure, Elvis, you can talk to me. I never talked to a dead guy before."

"Elvis? You've got me confused son, a lot of people make that mistake. I guess there is a resemblance. My name's John."

"OK, Elvis," the kid replied.

"Call me what you like," John said. "But I'd like to talk to you." He sat down next to the kid.

"Yeah, so?"

"Why are you smoking that marijuana cigarette?"

"Oh man, are you a cop?"

"No, son, I'm not a cop. I just want to talk to you about it."

"Then what are you, a priest or something? I'm not in the mood for some just-say-no bullshit."

"You shouldn't call it that."

"Why not?"

"First of all, because it's vulgar language. But I have to expect that from kids these days. But mostly because it's not bull. I've seen it enough in my life, son."

"My name's not son, Elvis."

"Well what is your name?"

"Dog."

"Dog?"

"Yeah. Dog."

"Your parents named you Dog?"

"No. They just treat me like one."

"What's your real name?"

"I won't tell you."

"Why not?"

"Because it's a stupid name and I hate it."

"How bad can it be?"

"Bad. Very bad."

"Bad enough to make you smoke that garbage to forget it?"

"Yeah, maybe it is."

"OK. I guess I'll call you Dog."

"It's my band name."

"Band name? You play in a band?"

"Yeah. I'm a bass player. I play in a heavy metal band. We're pretty lousy, but we're getting better."

"You seem young yet. How old are you?"

"Sixteen."

"So you've got a long time to get better. But is that all you do? Play in a band? Do you go to school?"

"See."

"See what?"

"I knew you were a priest."

"Now I'm not a priest. I'm just interested in you."

Dog stood up. He tossed the remainder of the joint into the river. He wouldn't look at John.

"What are you interested in me for? You a reporter or something? Doing a story about kids and drugs?"

"No, I'm nothing like that."

"Then what's with you, Elvis? Why should you care about me?"

"Because you seem like a young man in trouble. I'd like to try to help."

"Look, if you're Elvis, you can give me a million bucks. That'll be a big help. If you're not, get the hell out of here."

John sighed and looked at the river. He wondered if he'd be able to break through to this kid. Dog sat down next to him again.

"OK. I'll tell you," John said. "I am Elvis. Really."

"Sure, sure."

"But I'm not going to give you a million dollars, because it wouldn't do you any good. It would do you nothing but harm."

"So harm me, what the hell do I care?"

"What would you do with a million dollars, Dog?"

"I'd spend it. I'd buy a car. A lot of drugs and beer. Buy a house in the woods. And bring a bunch of hot women there and make them my slaves."

"Is that really all you'd do?"

"No."

"I thought so. What else would you do?"

"I'd have my parents killed."

Dog stood up again and walked about ten feet away. He picked up some small rocks and began tossing them into the river.

Elvis walked over to him. He began tossing rocks as well.

"Tell me, Dog. Where do you get those ideas?"

"They're just ideas. Everybody has those ideas."

"Everybody? Who's everybody?"

"All my friends. The guys in the band. We talk about it all the time. When we're rich and famous, we're gonna do just what I said I'd do."

"What if you never become rich and famous?"

"Then I don't."

For a minute or two, both were silent, just tossing rocks into the water.

"You hungry, Dog?"

"Yeah, I'm hungry."

"How about getting some hamburgers?"

"Sure. You paying?"

"I'm paying."

There was a fast-food restaurant on the river. The two went there, bought some food, and returned to where they were before.

The food seemed to loosen the boy's tongue. For a time, Elvis and the kid just joked around, making stupid remarks about nothing.

"So what's really your name, Dog?"

"I'm still not gonna tell you."

"OK, OK. You don't have to. But will you tell me why you were smoking that dope?"

"I don't know."

"You must know. You must have some reason."

"Because it makes me feel good, I guess."

"In what way?"

"Makes me forget everything."

"That's what I thought. That's why so many people turn to it."

"You know people on dope?"

"I have known them. Plenty of them, too. I was in show business Dog, you know that."

"Oh yeah. I keep forgetting you're really Elvis." Dog laughed when he said this.

"It seems innocent and simple enough when you begin," Elvis said. "But it hooks you in. It'll sneak up on you before you know it."

"Yeah, sure."

"But let's talk about something else. Is that a heavy metal group on your shirt?"

"Yeah."

"Why do you like that kind of music?"

"I don't know. It's cool."

"What makes it cool?"

"It's just cool."

"Is my music cool?"

Dog laughed at Elvis. "Your music? Cool? No way! Nobody listens to that stuff."

"Nobody *you* know, you mean."

"Yeah, what's the difference?"

"Well, if you don't know them it doesn't necessarily mean that there isn't anybody who . . ." Elvis noticed the wicked grin on Dog's face.

"You set me up for that one, didn't you, Dog?"

"Yeah. I did. Thanks for falling for it." He laughed again.

"Anytime. SON."

"Hey, don't call me son, Elvis!"

"OK, Dog, now get serious a minute here. I want to know, what do you like about that music?"

"It's cool. It's the sound and the words."

"You listen to the words?"

"All the time. They're bad."

"Bad?"

"I mean good bad. You know."

"What are they about?"

"Cool stuff. Like death. And sex."

"What makes death so cool?" Elvis asked, the passion rising in his voice. "I thought death was bad. I mean bad bad."

"It's other people dying that's cool. Songs about mass destruction, the end of world. Stuff like that."

"But don't you think it's a little strange that you enjoy something like that? Think about it a minute and answer me honestly."

Dog looked down at his feet and played with his shoe-laces for a moment.

"I don't know," he said slowly. "I guess it is, maybe."

"What draws you to it, Dog? Why are you attracted to death? Do you want to die?"

Dog was silent for a long while.

"Yeah. Sometimes I do."

"Why, Dog?"

"Because there's nothing worth living for. So maybe dying's better."

"Nothing worth living for?" Elvis shouted. "But you're

only sixteen! What do you know about what's worth living for?''

"There hasn't been much yet," Dog said blankly.

"But don't you want to do things? To go places? To accomplish something?''

"Yeah. I want to get rich."

"Rich," Elvis said, in a tsk-tsk voice.

"Yeah. Rich. Like you, Elvis, like you." There was bitterness in Dog's words.

Elvis blew air out of his pursed lips in frustration.

"I'm going to tell you something straight now, Dog. So you listen closely.

"First, I'm rich. And what has it gotten me? I'm supposed to be dead. I'm running around from place to place. My life is a mess. I can almost never see my own child. What the hell good has being rich been to me?''

"Yeah, but you got girls and . . . ''

"I said be quiet!" Elvis grew stern. "Girls. That's all any sixteen-year-old guy wants, I guess. I wasn't any different. But it's not like in the movies. It's not all sparks and fire. Sometimes it can be, sure, with someone you really love. But the rest is a lot of lies. Like the lies in those songs of yours.''

"They're not lies!" Dog was not going to stand for attacks on his music.

"Oh no?" Elvis shot back at him. "Somebody tells you it's great to see people die, and that's not a lie? Somebody tells you it's good to beat up women, and that's not a lie? Somebody tells you it's good to worship Satan, and that's not a lie?''

"No. It's not!"

Dog turned his face away. He seemed to be hiding it.

"Now come on, Dog, I didn't mean to yell at you," Elvis said with concern. "But look at what's in front of you!

"Answer one question for me.''

"I already did!" It was clear that Dog was crying and trying to hide it.

"Well then just answer it to yourself. Since you started listening to your heavy metal, do things in your life seem better or worse?"

A long silence followed.

"Dog?" Elvis asked. "You have any answer to that?"

"No," Dog said quietly.

"You mean, no, you have no answer, or no, because you don't want to say your answer?"

"I don't know."

"I believe you don't know," Elvis said, as he put his hand on Dog's shoulder.

"Listen, buddy, I'm not trying to upset you. I'm just trying to get you to see things differently.

"It's pretty clear you don't have much meaning to your life. You don't know what you want or where you're going. But that's all been fed into you. It's not you. It's what everybody else is telling you to believe! The records, the movies, television. Everywhere you look, people are telling you that nothing matters except having fun or getting girls or goofing off. Nobody tells you about working hard, about being proud of yourself, about making yourself into a man."

"A man?"

"Yes, a man. And it's got nothing to do with women. You don't need a woman to be a man."

"What do I need?"

"Nothing. Just yourself. You have everything you need."

"How do I know what to do?"

"Did you ever try to ask anyone?"

"Like who?"

"Like your mom and dad?"

"I hate them."

"Why?"

"I don't know."

"You don't know? Don't you think that's a pretty ridiculous answer?"

"Yeah."

"Well if you don't know, I do. You hate them because you've been told to hate them. Because you're a teenager and everybody tells you you're supposed to hate them. Because they try to make you go the right way and you resent it, so you think you hate them.

"You know, when I first started singing, parents hated me. They thought I was turning their kids away from the good path into something dangerous and wicked. And there may be some truth to that. But it wasn't because I wanted it that way, it was because people interpreted it that way and *said* that's what I meant. But Elvis Presley never meant turning away from your parents. I loved my parents and I still do, even though they've passed away.

"Elvis Presley never meant being bad, or turning to sex. Sure, I was a sex symbol. Girls went crazy over me. But girls have always gone crazy over singers. What I was about was something else. It wasn't about sex. It was about freedom. Freedom to be what you were best at. I hate the way people turned it all around for their own purposes."

"So why didn't you stop them?"

"Because I was young and foolish. A lot like you, I'd expect. I was taken advantage of by a lot of people. It was all happening so fast, I didn't even realize it. It wasn't until years later that I was able to take stock and see what I had done. A lot of what Elvis Presley led to, I don't like at all. But I didn't mean for any of that to happen.

"It's just that sometimes things get out of your control. You have to be very careful about that."

The river rolled by. Both man and boy were deep in thought.

"Hey, Dog."

"Yeah, Elvis?"

"You ever been up in that arch?"

"No."

85

"No! You live in St. Louis and you've never been in the arch?"

"I just never got around to it."

"Well you're getting around to it now. Let's go."

"You paying?"

"I'm paying."

Elvis and the kid walked over to the arch. On the way, Dog was reciting heavy metal lyrics to Elvis, who again and again said, "I can't believe they let them put that in a song! What's happened to the world?"

They sat in the unusual gondolalike elevator that carried them to the top of the Gateway Arch.

"It's quite a sight from up there, Dog," Elvis said on the way to the top of the arch. "It's inspiring."

"Maybe I'll write a song about it." Dog grinned. "About all these people falling off the arch and dying."

"Dog!"

"Just kidding," he laughed. "I don't know if that's such a good idea anymore."

They made it to the top. They walked out. When Dog saw the view, he was stunned.

"Man. That view is bad."

"You mean good bad?"

"*Very* good bad."

They looked and looked, staring out over the great nation that stretched endlessly before them.

"What are you thinking about, Dog?" Elvis asked.

"I don't know. Nothing, I guess. And everything."

"Like what?"

"Well, like this. There were people who built this thing, right? I mean, somebody had the idea to build this, right?"

"Yes. Go on."

"So what a great idea! I mean, a giant arch. A giant arch that people can go up inside of. How do you think of something like that?"

"It's just an idea, Dog. There's lots of good ideas out there. People have them every day."

"I want to have a good idea someday," Dog said, while his eyes feasted on the view. "I want to do something like this."

"Why?"

"Because. Don't you see? This is something." Dog spoke with great excitement. It was the thrilling voice of self-discovery. "This arch will be here for like a thousand years probably. Everybody knows it. People come from all over to see it. It means something. It really means something."

"What's it mean to you?"

"To me? Well, it's called the Gateway Arch, right?"

"Yeah."

"So that means it leads somewhere, or it opens up onto something, right? It's like a gate. You go through it and you're someplace else. You're not inside anymore, you're outside."

"And what does that mean to you?"

"It means you're someplace new. It means you're at a place where everything is different. A place where you can start all over again. It's like, you walk through this gate and you get a whole new life. You can get it right this time."

"Do you think you can get it right this time?"

Dog hesitated a moment as he looked down at the Mississippi.

"Elvis?"

"Yeah, Dog?"

"A lot of people died on that river, didn't they?"

"I expect so."

"But most of them died trying to do something. Working, or going someplace. They were getting something done when they died, right?"

Dog spoke with a kind of earnest feeling that he hadn't known in years.

"In most cases, probably so."

"But they didn't know they were going to die. And they

87

probably didn't want to die. They probably wanted to die less than anything."

"True."

"But they died anyway. They died for something and they didn't want to. So how can I want to die for nothing?"

"Do you really want to die, Dog?"

Dog's eyes took in the vast expanse before him.

"No. No, Elvis, I don't. I don't want to. Not anymore." There was conviction in his words.

"Good. I'm glad to hear that, Dog, I'm really glad to hear that."

Elvis put his arm around the boy's shoulder as they looked out the windows together.

"Elvis?"

"Yes?"

"I'll tell you a secret."

"What's that?"

"My name. My name's Augie. That's why they call me Dog. Augie Doggie."

"Augie?"

"Yeah."

"Well, that's not such a bad name . . ."

"Hey, don't lie to me, man. You've been pretty honest so far. Don't lie now."

Elvis gave a short, quiet laugh at himself. The boy had seen through him so easily.

"Yeah, you're right. You got stuck with one lousy name."

"But you know what?" Dog said, emotion choking his voice. "I don't care about it. It's just a name. This could be called the Garbage Arch instead of the Gateway Arch, and it would still be just as great."

Elvis smiled at the boy's new wisdom.

"Elvis, can we do one more thing?"

"Sure. What is it?"

"Let's go down now. I want to walk under the arch. I want to walk through it. I want to walk through the gate."

"You got it."

They took the elevator down. They walked outside and stood on one side of the arch, looking through it toward the river.

"Know what Elvis? When I walk under that arch, nothing's going to be the same anymore. It's the gateway to everything. It'll all be different."

"You think so, Dog?"

"Yeah. I know so. . . . John." An edge of doubt crept back into Dog's voice.

"John? Why are you calling me John?"

"Because that's your name. C'mon, you're not really Elvis. Elvis is dead."

"Maybe he is and maybe he isn't," Elvis said. "There are other gateways in this world, Dog, gateways not many people know about."

Dog looked at Elvis for a long time. He just stared at his face.

"You really mean that?"

"Would I lie to you, son?"

"No. I don't think so. And I'm still not your son."

"Well, stop stalling now you little punk!" The words were spoken with great affection, and Dog knew it. "Get your tail through that arch, Dog!"

"OK, Elvis-John, whoever you are. I'm going."

Dog started to walk.

"Don't walk, Dog!" Elvis called. "Run! Run through! Run to your freedom! Don't wait a minute more!"

Dog turned to him with a look of exhilaration on his face.

"You're right, Elvis!" he shouted. "Enough time's been wasted. I'm going!"

Dog took off as fast as he could run. As he passed under the arch he raised his hands in triumph. He kept running, until he was almost at the river.

He turned around.

"Hey, Elvis! I feel like . . ." His voice stopped short. Elvis was gone.

"Elvis? Hey, Elvis? Where'd you go?"

Dog looked for over half an hour. He never found Elvis again.

The day was coming to a close. The sun was setting. Dog was at the river. He was sitting on the shore, thinking about the day, thinking about what he had learned, how he had changed.

It really is different now, he thought. *I gotta stop being such a jerk with my life. I think I'll go home and tell Mom I'm going to cut my hair. No, that might kill her! I'll break her in slow and maybe do some homework while she's looking. But that might kill her too. Well, I'll just have to take that chance.*

Dog stood up. It had been a long day. He glanced over his shoulder at the Gateway Arch. He was glad he lived in the city with the arch because it would always be there to remind him. He would walk through it again and again, whenever he needed the inspiration, whenever he felt a little short of hope.

Well, it was time to go home.

He started walking away. He put his hands in his pockets and he felt something. He took it out. It was a joint. He had one left.

He took out a match and lit the joint.

He watched it burn for a moment.

"Burn, baby, burn," he said.

With a flick of his fingers, he tossed it into the river. He turned and headed home. He never looked back.

THE PAPER TRAIL OF
JOHN BURROWS

One piece of evidence frequently cited by those who feel Elvis Presley is alive is the mysterious trail of John Burrows.

"John Burrows" (sometimes spelled "Burroughs") was an alias Elvis frequently used before his reputed death in 1977. Oddly enough, the name is still in use. No one is sure why.

A computer hacker—one of those people who are skilled at gaining access to information through a computer—became interested in the question of whether or not Elvis was alive. He decided to try and track him through credit reports. Virtually every adult in the country who uses a credit card or pays bills can be located in a credit report. These reports are compiled continually and they are often difficult to obtain.

The hacker first typed in Elvis Presley's name. The computer showed that no records were available. Then the hacker typed in Elvis's social security number. This is where it gets interesting.

The computer listed an extensive credit report. The report doesn't show what purchases are made; it only records that some financial activity is taking place under a certain name or number. And next to Elvis Presley's social security number was another social security number. The hacker entered this number into the computer, and this time a name did come up: the name was Elvis Presley.

It seems that somehow the name or number of Elvis Presley is very actively making financial transactions. What adds to the mystery is that throughout the credit report the name of John Burrows appears. Elvis Presley and John Burrows are linked again and again.

This would not be unusual if these were old records. But credit reports are all destroyed seven years after a person dies. This information was being uncovered in 1991, fourteen years after Presley's reported death. Furthermore, the most recent transaction then noted took place in March of 1991. The reports cannot tell us who is using these names and numbers, but there is no question that someone is using them and the name and social security number of Elvis Presley are very active, even fourteen years after his death.

The credit reports allow us to make one further observation. The locations of the transactions can be traced. We start with a record of a transaction made by John Burrows in Fort Worth, Texas, in December, 1989. This "paper trail" then leads us through Kalamazoo, Michigan; Little Rock, Arkansas; Birmingham, Alabama; Shreveport, Louisiana; Kansas City, Missouri; Perrysburg, Ohio; and Chicago, Illinois. Interestingly, many of these states are frequent sites of Elvis sightings. But the most interesting aspect of the paper trail is where it begins. The first record stems from 3764 Elvis Presley Boulevard in Memphis, Tennessee. That is the address of Graceland.

What conclusions can be drawn from this? There are three possibilities.

First, someone may have concocted a fake credit record in order to create the story that Elvis Presley is alive. Why someone would do this and who it might be is something we cannot know.

Second, someone may be illegally using Elvis Presley's social security number and financial records for his or her own gain. The credit report may be a smokescreen designed to make it harder to locate the culprit.

The third possibility is the simplest: Elvis Presley is alive.

A MAGICAL MOMENT

Lake George, New York.

It was the summer of 1990, and Sherry was back at Lake George, a fun-filled resort town in northern New York State. She was seventeen years old, and this was her seventh visit. Her parents took Sherry and her brother there each year. They rented a cabin and stayed for two weeks. This year was special for Sherry because, for the first time, her parents permitted her to bring her best friend, Charisse. There were so many things to show her, and they weren't going to waste a minute.

It was on their fourth day of seeing the sights that they had their encounter with Elvis. Sherry and Charisse liked Elvis, though they were not devoted fans. Like most people their age, they preferred more contemporary music. Most of Sherry's friends didn't care the least about Elvis, but Sherry's father was a big fan and had dozens of albums. That's how Sherry knew about Elvis. Charisse listened to Elvis because Sherry did, and she grew to like him too.

Their story begins in one of Lake George's wax museums. While no match for Madame Tussaud's famous London wax exhibit, the museums at Lake George were still frightening fun, as customers made their way through darkened, twisting hallways that opened up onto clever scenes that more often than not were gruesome or violent in nature. The halls were usually filled with screams and giggles from visitors whose horror always turned quickly to hilarity.

Sherry and Charisse were making their way through the museum, mostly laughing at the scenes of beheadings, gruesome murders, and misshapen faces. There were some celebrity figures as well. These weren't frightening, but instead produced the same response from almost everybody: "How do they get them to look so lifelike?" On occasion, when the artist had not done his job so efficiently, the alternate response would be laughter and a derisive "That doesn't look anything like him!"

Sherry was a big movie buff, and she liked to linger over the celebrity portrayals. Charisse got a bit bored, as she preferred the horror scenes. There was one exception for Sherry, however. This was the wax portrayal of Elvis Presley. Sherry didn't like that one at all because it always made her sad. She still remembered the day Elvis Presley died because her father cried when he heard the news. She had never seen him cry before, and it upset her terribly at the time. It is one of her earliest memories, one of the few things she remembers from so long ago.

Sherry had been through the wax museum so often that she knew it by heart. She knew what was coming around every corner, and she used her knowledge to try to frighten Charisse. But as they approached the Elvis scene, Sherry stopped playing her games. She told Charisse that she hoped Charisse wouldn't mind if they walked quickly past this one, and she told Charisse why. Charisse felt for her friend, and she agreed to pass Elvis by if it would make Sherry feel better.

"I hate that Elvis dummy," Sherry said. "I can't help it, but every time I see it I can hear my daddy crying."

Charisse, not knowing what to say, brought up something she had heard on television.

"You know some people say he's still alive, that he didn't really die and it's all a hoax."

"I know," Sherry said. "My father bought one of those books about it, and I looked through it a little. He doesn't believe it, though, and I don't either. It's too crazy."

"Wouldn't it be weird if it were true, though?" Charisse said.

They were about to turn the corner to where the Elvis model was, when Sherry grabbed Charisse's arm and pulled her back.

"Did you hear that?" she whispered.

"Hear what? I didn't hear anything."

"That voice. It sounded like Elvis Presley."

"Get out of here," Charisse said. "You're just trying to scare me again."

"No, I'm not. I wouldn't kid around about this one. Listen . . ."

They both held their breaths. Sure enough, they heard voices from around the corner. It was hard to make out, since people behind them in the corridor were screaming and laughing loudly. But it seemed to be two people talking about the Elvis model, and one of them sounded a lot like Elvis Presley.

"Ain't that the most ridiculous thing?" the Elvis voice said. "They just didn't get it right. I never wore a ring like that in my life. And those shoes are way off!" He and his companion both laughed.

Sherry was shaking.

"My God," she said. "It's him. He's alive."

"No way," Charisse said. "It's just some guy kidding around. Maybe one of the Elvis impersonators. Isn't there one who does a show at that bar down the street?"

Yes, thought Sherry, there was. She had forgotten about

that. She was surprised at herself, because she had seen that show many times. Her father went three or four times during each vacation because he enjoyed it so. Sherry had seen it five times in the past few years. That was the answer, she thought. *It's just the impersonator.*

No longer nervous, she and Charisse turned the corner. As soon as she saw him, she pulled back. She pushed Charisse back around the corner. They hadn't been seen.

"It's him!" Sherry said, her voice shaking. "I mean, it's not him. The impersonator. It's not him! I've seen him before and he's young! This Elvis is old! It's not the impersonator!"

"No way!" Charisse said. "That's crazy. It's gotta be some other impersonator!"

"No, it's not!" Sherry whispered. "I'm telling you it's him, it's Elvis. He *is* alive! That's why he's talking about the dummy that way!"

The two girls were paralyzed. They didn't know what to do. They listened as Elvis and his companion joked more about the dummy. Then the man with Elvis asked him, jokingly, to sing to the dummy. "Show him who the real King is," he said.

And Elvis sang.

He sang a few lines from "Love Me Tender." His voice was beautiful, just the way Sherry had heard it on all those records. But it only lasted half a minute before Elvis broke up laughing.

Sherry knew for sure now it was really Elvis. She had to see him again.

She slowly turned the corner, trying to stay hidden in the dark. She stood there a moment, unseen, and stared at Elvis. He was older, and a little heavy, but it was unmistakably he. The light from the display shone on his face and she saw clearly.

Then the man with Elvis saw her watching them.

"C'mon," he said to Elvis. "We'd better get going."

Elvis turned back and saw Sherry. She had tears in her eyes, and her lips were quivering.

Elvis looked a little downcast as he started to walk away.

"Wait, Elvis!" Sherry said, the words almost lost in her throat. "Please!"

His companion tried to pull him away, but there was something in the girl's voice which Elvis couldn't turn away from.

He stepped closer to Sherry. "Yes, darling?" he said, his voice full of tenderness.

"Just tell me," Sherry said. "Just tell me . . . is it you? Is it really you?"

Elvis hesitated a moment. Again, his companion called to him. "Let's go! C'mon!"

Elvis looked at him. He took a step backward. Sherry thought he would leave without another word.

But he stopped again. Looking Sherry right in the eye, he told her what she longed to hear.

"Yes, darling, it's me. But do me a favor and don't tell anybody. Is that a deal?"

Sherry's heart was pounding so hard she could barely reply.

"Yes," she whispered. "It's a deal."

"I knew I could trust you," Elvis said. Then he turned to go.

But for the last time, he hesitated. He turned quickly back to Sherry. He stepped over to where she was standing and he kissed her on the cheek.

"Good-bye, darling," he said.

Then he walked quickly away, turned the corner, and was gone.

Sherry fell back against the wall and slumped to the ground. In an instant, Charisse was by her side.

"Oh my God," she was saying. "Oh my God, that was him! That was him! And he spoke to you! And he kissed you! Oh my God!"

Sherry couldn't move. For at least fifteen minutes she

sat there in the dark corner, staring at the wax model. *Was it all a dream?* she asked herself. *But Charisse saw it too. It must be real.*

Other people passed by the two of them, some giving them funny looks. But Sherry didn't care. She couldn't leave this spot. Not yet. This had been the most amazing moment of her life, and she went over it in her mind again and again. She wanted to make sure she never forgot a single detail. Ten times she asked Charisse what Elvis had said, the exact words. Each time, Charisse gave her the same answers. Sherry knew the words were correct, but she couldn't hear them often enough.

"Did he really call me darling?" she'd ask, over and over. "Did he really kiss me? Did he really say it was him?"

Charisse said yes and yes and yes again. Sherry didn't tire of asking, and Charisse didn't tire of answering. This was a special moment that the two best friends shared together. Sherry knew deep in her heart that whatever else might happen between her and Charisse in the future, they would always have this moment. Fifty years from now she could call Charisse on the phone and say, "Remember when we saw Elvis?" and the whole thing would come flooding back.

At that moment, sitting there with her closest friend holding her hand, Sherry wondered if she would ever recover from it. She felt as though she'd walk through life in a daze, always waiting for reality to return, yet it never would.

She might never have left that museum had Charisse not urged her up. Together they walked through the rest of the museum, ignoring all the sights around them. When they stepped out into the light of day, Sherry felt a change in herself. That moment, which had been so brilliant and diffuse, a blazing white light inside her, now solidified. It took on a new form, less bright perhaps, but stronger and deeper. She knew now that reality would be reality, as it always had been. Elvis would not get in her way in life. He would not be the giant presence she felt in the dark of the museum, blocking out everything else. No, it would be different.

Elvis would stay with her forever. But he would be part of her, not something beyond her or above her. And that was how it should be, how he would want it. *That was why he kissed me,* she thought. *Without that touch, it wouldn't be real enough. It would be a dream moment that I could never awaken from. He knew that. He knew the kiss would make it real; the kiss would take the dream and wrap it up in a bundle, tucked away inside me.*

And that, she says, is where it remains. A magical moment stored in her heart, a moment when a wild dream-vision of Elvis Presley became forever real, when it reached out to her and kissed her, there in the wax museum, in a corner, in the dark.

This photo of Elvis was taken only three months before his death. Witnesses at his funeral reported that the body in the coffin looked "much younger." *(Wide World Photos)*

On August 16, 1977, a Memphis Funeral Home hearse removed Elvis' body from the Baptist Memorial Hospital. The next day, when the gates of Graceland were opened to the public, over 20,000 people passed in front of the coffin in less than four hours.

(Wide World Photos)

Thousands of people lined the blocks around Graceland after the news got out. Over the course of two days it was estimated that over 80,000 people came from all parts of the country to pay their respects.   *(Wide World Photos)*

A string of white funeral vehicles moves along Elvis Presley Boulevard on its way to the Forest Hills Cemetery in Memphis.

(Wide World Photos)

On the historical marker:

4E 77
ELVIS ARON PRESLEY

Elvis Presley was born in Tupelo, Mississippi
on January 8, 1935, the son of Vernon and
Gladys Presley. He moved to Memphis in 1948.
Soon after signing a contract with Sun Records
in 1954 he achieved tremendous popularity. His
musical and acting career in records, movies,
television, and concerts made him one of the
most successful and outstanding entertainers
in the world. He died on August 16, 1977 and is
buried here at his Memphis home, Graceland.

This photo of Graceland was taken in March of 1992. Note the correct spelling of Aron on the historical marker.

(Wide World Photos)

This photo of Elvis' father, Vernon, placing a rose on his son's grave provides a very good look at the mysterious Aaron grave-marker. What is the significance of this misspelling?

(Wide World Photos)

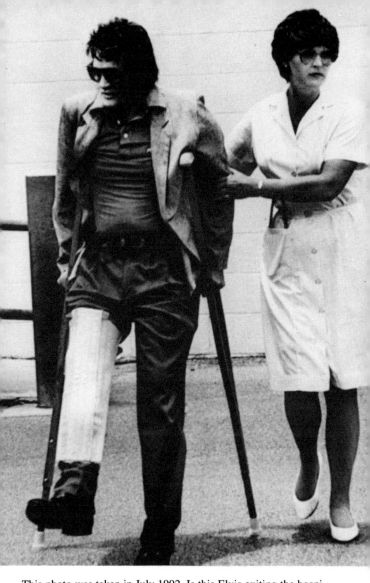

This photo was taken in July 1992. Is this Elvis exiting the hospital after a motorcycle accident? *(Weekly World News)*

This photo is from May 1992. Could this be The King?

(Weekly World News)

WISE WORDS ON
THE TRAIL

The Appalachian Trail.

For two weeks, Scott had been hiking the Appalachian Trail. He was heading for the highest point on the trail, Mt. Mitchell, in North Carolina, 6,684 feet high. Another day or two and he'd be there.

The hiking had been tough going. Scott wasn't in such great shape. But the thinking had been even tougher.

Scott had been through a messy divorce a few months earlier. Things had not gone well with him since. He made good money at his job selling computer security packages, but the work bored him. The divorce had made him realize how empty so much of his life was. He had spent the ten years since college in a wild binge of acquisitiveness, buying the best of everything. He had all the things that other people envied: a top-rated sports car; a beautiful home in an exclusive area, complete with a pool and tennis court; membership in the ritziest country club in the state; and a beautiful wife.

Yes, Cheryl was beautiful. And just as successful as Scott, having made partner in her law firm, the youngest person ever to do so in that rich, old establishment. Together, they were the model Yuppie couple. They gave parties that spared no expense, took vacations in the classiest European locales. They lived the life-style of the rich and famous. It all seemed like a dream to Scott, who had grown up in a lower middle-class, blue-collar household where there never seemed to be enough money to fix the car or repair the back porch.

But it all went bust over kids. Scott wanted them. Cheryl didn't.

After six years of marriage and fun, Scott wanted to begin a family. Cheryl had always said she would have children when the time was right, it just never seemed to be right. Scott didn't want to wait much longer, so he began to push Cheryl on the subject. For over a year she claimed that work pressures wouldn't permit her to get pregnant now. She had to make partner first. Then she made partner, and all that changed was her excuse. Now she was too busy as a partner.

One dark and bitter night it all came out. They had given a small dinner party for five or six friends. At about 2:30 A.M. the last guests had departed, and Scott and Cheryl were getting ready for bed. One of the couples at the party had announced that they were expecting their first child, so Scott brought up the subject of children again. Cheryl, who had been drinking a bit too much that evening and undergoing great strain at work, turned on him and admitted that she didn't want children, not then or ever. They fought back and forth, all their repressed rage coming to the fore. Accusations were made that evening that could never be forgiven or forgotten. Cheryl admitted to an affair she had had a few years earlier. Scott admitted to one as well. Six years of secrets and denials were dragged into the open. The battle went on and on until the rising of the sun, when both fighters were too exhausted to continue. By that point, the damage had been done. Like barbarian invaders who aimlessly set fire to everything in their path, Scott and Cheryl let nothing escape the all-consuming torch. That day, the sun rose on a blackened wasteland, a burned and charred remnant of the happy couple, the couple everybody envied. It was all over, and over forever.

The legal battle was equally bitter, Cheryl using her lawyer's skills to contest everything, even things Scott knew she didn't care about. She was seeking the final victory in the battle, and Scott let her have it. He didn't have enough left inside to care anymore.

After everything had tumbled down and the rubble had settled, Scott found himself alone in a small apartment, his friends mostly gone (they had sided with his wife), his savings pillaged, and with a future that seemed to lead nowhere. He still had his job, and even after alimony payments he made a lot of money, but it all felt insignificant now. What had it all gotten him, the car, the house, the best of everything? Was *this* where it all led, to lonely nights haunted by desperate memories? There had to be more than this to life; there had to be something out there that meant something, that mattered. Scott needed to find himself, to crawl out from under the refuse of the past six years, which lay on him like dirt on a grave.

With no idea where to turn, he decided he'd turn to himself. He'd get away for a few weeks, go into the hills and walk part of the Appalachian Trail. He had never done such a thing before, and he'd probably make a mess of it, but he didn't care. At least it was something to do, something to strive for. The preparations alone gave him what he needed most: something to think about other than the past. When at last he arrived at the trail and started to hike, he knew he'd made the right decision. Maybe he wouldn't find any answers up in the hills, maybe things would be just as empty as always when he returned, but he had to do something or he'd go crazy, and this felt right.

This was the background that eventuated in Scott, the rich Yuppie, roughing it in the hills of North Carolina.

Mt. Mitchell was his goal. Scott wanted to get up as high as he could just to stare out over the world and think about it all. And he wanted to rest there for a day or two as well because his body was more sore than it had ever been in his life.

He made camp early that evening. He could have pushed on a little farther, but he wasn't in a hurry and the night was going to be very clear. Scott thought he would lie out and look up at the stars. Maybe he'd see a shooting star and he could make a wish. Trouble was, he didn't know what to wish for.

The sun was going down when he heard someone coming along the trail. This wasn't unusual since Scott was about as slow a hiker as you could find. Several people had passed him along the way, and he hadn't paid them any mind. But now he found himself wishing for someone to talk to. For two weeks he hadn't spoken to anyone.

He made up his mind to speak to whoever was coming. When he saw the man, Scott was a bit surprised. He looked a lot like Elvis Presley. Of course, this was ridiculous. *A lot of people look like that,* Scott thought, *so what's the big deal. He looks like Elvis Presley. I can live with that.*

Scott called to him. They exchanged a few casual remarks, when Scott decided to invite the man to join him.

"Say," he said, "I know this may sound a little strange, but I'd really like it if you could stop a while, maybe join me for dinner. I haven't talked to anyone in two weeks. I guess I'm just lonely for some company."

"You know, I was feeling about the same," the man said. "I get lonely a lot in my life, even though there's almost always someone around me. I came on the trail to get away for a little while, but I could use some company myself tonight."

"Well I haven't really introduced myself yet," Scott said. "My name's Scott J."

"My name's John," the man said. "John Burrows."

"So, John, how about we get a little supper started?

I've got a bunch of freeze-dried crap with me. You can have whatever you want. I don't care, it all tastes like garbage to me.''

And so the conversation went. For an hour or so, they occupied themselves making dinner, talking about the trail, about the food, about Mt. Mitchell. It wasn't until the first stars started to appear that Scott ventured into deeper waters.

He began to talk about his divorce. He really hadn't talked to anyone about it before, at least not in any detail. He didn't know why he was telling it all to a stranger, but the man seemed very understanding, as if he knew all about problems and the pain that life can bring.

It was already well into the night when Scott finished.

"God, I guess I've been doing all the talking here," he said, a little embarrassed at how emotional he had been.

"That's all right," John said. "I know how it feels to have a story inside that you need to tell, but there's no one you can tell it to. I've got some things inside myself, but I have to keep them there. It's not an easy feeling, is it?''

"Well, I'll be happy to listen," Scott said. "I don't think I'll be much help, since I can't even get my own life straight, but if you want to talk, I'm going to be here all night.''

"No, thanks just the same. I'd like to talk about it, really I would. I think you'd even understand. But it's just something I can't talk about. It's nothing to do with you, understand. I wish I could explain it more, but it's better that I don't.''

"OK, if that's the way it is," Scott said. "But if you change your mind, just let me know.''

After this, they both fell quiet for a while. Scott and John were lying back, staring at stars. Suddenly, a shooting star passed over them.

"Hey, look at that!" Scott said. "I've been waiting to see one every night, and this is the first time!''

"Don't forget to make a wish," John said.

"A wish . . . A wish . . . I don't know what to wish for," Scott said, with great sadness in his voice.

"I wished for something," John replied, and sadness was in his voice as well. "But you know you can't tell a wish because it won't come true."

"No problem here," Scott said, "since I didn't wish anything anyway."

Another moment of silence followed.

"John?" Scott said, breaking the quiet. "Do you know much about life?"

"Life? I don't really know if I do. I've lived an awful lot of life, for sure. More than most people. But I don't think I've figured it all out. It certainly is a topic I've thought about a lot though."

"Really? Have you? I've never thought about it at all, to be honest. At least not until recently. I mean, just basic questions. Like look at those stars. They're so beautiful, so far away. The universe is so huge. But what does it all mean? Where did it come from? What *is* it, even? What the hell is the universe? I don't know. I simply don't know."

"Well let me ask you a question," John said. "I don't want to pry into anything personal, but I think it's a question you have to ask yourself. Would you mind?"

"Hell, there's nothing personal I haven't already told you! No, I don't mind. Ask me whatever you want. I've got nothing to hide."

"It's this: Do you believe in God?"

"God? Jesus, that's a weird question."

John laughed at Scott's rather peculiar response.

Scott laughed too. "I mean, it's weird to me, I guess. It's probably not a weird question for most people, for normal people, but I've lived my life so separate from anything having to do with God, at least since I was a teenager, that it just seems weird to me. I never thought about God. My wife never did. Nobody I knew ever said anything about religion. You just don't, not in the social circles I was in. You'd talk about religion like it was a race. You'd make jokes about it, like 'Oh, he's just a cheap Jew,' or 'What do you expect from her, she's a Catholic.' Insults, really. That's all religion was for my friends and me, just another way to put someone down.''

John paused in thought for a moment.

"I see. I've known plenty of people like you, Scott. Don't think you're so unusual. It's a godless world. And that's our biggest problem.''

"You think so? I've thought about things like that sometimes, like when I was in college and you'd talk about stuff like that. But I always thought religion was a good way to keep the peasants content, you know, so they wouldn't attack the royalty. I guess I considered myself among the royalty. Religion was something for them, not for me. I didn't have the time for it.''

"And look where's it's gotten you. Tell me this much, do you think if you and your wife had been believers, real believers, you would have ended up the way you did? Do you think she would have been so dead set against children?''

Scott didn't know how to respond to this.

"I don't want to be insulting,'' John apologized. "Please don't take it wrong. But I know you're someone struggling with your life, and someone has to ask you some hard questions. I know you understand the notion that hard work leads to success and rewards. You've lived that for ten years. But it doesn't just apply to making money. Understanding your life is hard work too, and sometimes you have to go through some pain.''

"No pain, no gain,'' Scott said, his voice a blank. The phrase was one he used to use when he was working his way up, pushing himself, slaving away at crazy hours, flying from city to city selling his products, living on the adrenaline edge of near-collapse, pushing himself on and on for money, money, money. "No pain, no gain.'' How different it was now. He never knew then what true pain was. Now he understood, and he understood something deeper. His pain had just begun. There was more pain to come, but it was necessary pain. He had to confront it, or he'd be lost forever. But he couldn't confront it alone because he didn't know where to begin. Maybe John was his salvation. This stranger on the mountain, this man with a past he couldn't explain: maybe he was the sounding board Scott needed.

"No pain, no gain," Scott said it again.

"It's the truth," John said. "I've been through it myself. But you haven't answered my question yet, Scott. Do you believe in God or not?"

Scott paused in thought. "To be honest, John, no, I don't think I do. I'm not positive though. I was raised a Protestant, and that stuff sort of sticks with you, I guess, so I won't say no positively. But I don't think I do. Deep down, I don't think I believe in God."

"Well then, how do you explain the universe, Scott?"

"Ah, it's just scientific stuff. The Big Bang, or whatever they call it. It just came out of this big explosion, that's all. There's no God involved."

"Yeah, it's all so simple, isn't it? Well I've got a simple question for you, Scott. See if you can answer this. OK, I'll give you the Big Bang. The universe came out of a giant explosion. I think I even believe that myself. But answer this: what was it, exactly, that exploded? And how did it get there?"

"Well . . . it exploded, that's all. It was just this thing, out in space, that . . . well . . . that exploded!"

John laughed. "I think you realize how silly your answer just sounded, don't you?"

"Yeah," Scott laughed. "I guess I didn't say much of anything, did I? Oh hell, John, I don't *know* what the hell exploded or where the hell it came from! Shit, I don't even know what I'm going to be doing tomorrow! Don't ask me about the universe."

"OK, I won't," John said. "But do you mind if I tell you about it?"

"Mind? Of course not. I'd love to know."

"All right then. Let me tell you what I think. You don't have to accept any of this, and I'm not certain myself. But I've thought and read a lot over the years about this. Religion, the spiritual side of life, has always been a passion of mine. Maybe you won't believe what I believe, but it should give you a place to start thinking, and I think that's what you really need.

"I see things this way. The first thing we need to understand is the nature of things, the nature of the universe. It's like you were saying, looking up at the stars. Where does it all come from? What does it all mean?

"It all comes from God. And God is good. He's perfect and never changing. Yet the universe is full of change and imperfection and problems. Nevertheless, both of these realities exist at the same time. And they have always existed. God is eternal. He existed before the universe, before the Big Bang or whatever brought about creation. God was always there."

"Now wait a second," Scott interrupted. "That's one of those things I've never understood. How could God be eternal? I asked that once when I was a kid and nobody gave me a good answer. If everything comes from something, where does God come from? Was there a Mr. and Mrs. God?"

"That's a significant question. I had trouble with that one myself for a time. But I think I can explain it to you."

John turned toward Scott. His talking was becoming more animated. He began to punctuate his speech with hand gestures.

"As I said, God is eternal. He existed before time because God invented time. That's the key. There was no such thing as time before God invented it. He existed in a universe, if that's the right word, or some kind of plane of being, that was there before such a thing as time. As humans we can't conceive of life without time. How can such a thing be? But God isn't human, of course, and the notion of time doesn't apply to Him.''

"That's just so weird," Scott said, shaking his head. "How can someone, or something, exist outside of time?"

"It's hard to grasp because you have no connection to it. Try to think of it this way. Imagine you were a fish, one that lived deep under the sea. Now all your life you live in the sea, and you have no idea that there is any world other than the sea. You don't know that there is an entire world up above the sea. You know that light comes from above, but that's all.

"Then one day, you're caught in a net, and you get carried out of the water. All of a sudden you see an entire world that you never knew was there. In fact, you could never even conceive of a world without water because you had never seen such a thing. That's sort of the situation we're in. I can talk about a place without time, but you can't feel it in your bones because there's nothing to compare it to. But you can think it, even if you can't feel it, and it does make sense.''

"I still don't get it. So how did God get there? Nothing was before Him?"

"No, nothing was before Him, because there's no such thing as before or after in God's realm. There's only now. It's always been now for God. I don't even think God knows what came before, or where He came from. That's an even stranger question. Can even God know where He came from?

"It's just too abstract to comprehend fully. It's like the idea of infinity. You can say the universe is infinite, that it goes on forever. But what does that mean? How can anything go on forever? It's beyond our grasp. We just don't have the capacity to understand these things, except in the simplest terms.

"But let's accept that God was always there, and He created everything. Don't forget, either, that creation is still going on. It's a continual process. People think of creation as something that happened billions of years ago and is now over. But it's not over. Things are constantly being created. The universe is constantly evolving.''

"Well, I have another question," Scott said. "This whole creation thing. I'll accept, for now, that God created everything. Fine. That's not a problem. But let's get a little pickier. How do we even know this stuff really exists? How do I know this mountain we're on is really here? Or those stars in the sky are there? Those trees? Maybe it's just all in our minds. Maybe it's all some kind of dream."

"Yes, that's another tough question. There's an old Chinese story about a man who dreams he's a butterfly, but when he wakes up, he wonders if he's a butterfly dreaming about being a man."

"Jesus . . ." Scott muttered. "Maybe I'm just a bad dream my wife had. Or maybe it's the other way around! That wouldn't be too bad."

"Let's just hope she doesn't wake up," John chuckled. "I'm enjoying this conversation and I wouldn't want you to disappear on me!"

"That's OK. Don't worry, my wife didn't wake up once in six years, she's not gonna wake up now."

"Some dreams you'd like to awaken from."

"That's for sure. But get back to the point. What about the guy dreaming he's a butterfly?"

John paused a moment to gather his thoughts.

"You could say that the world is just an idea we have in our heads, that nothing else is here. People have said that in the past. Important philosophers, religious people. And technically you can't disprove it. Whatever I might say, you could just say 'It's all in my head.' And I can't get inside your head to prove you wrong. I can't get inside my own head, either, so there's no way to disprove it when somebody says everything's a dream or everything's just in your mind.

"But I think we have to depend on feelings here. On gut-level feelings. Look at this."

John reached over and picked up a small stick from the ground. He bent it in his hands until it snapped.

"Now what just happened? Was that an idea that I broke, or was it a real stick? Everything in you tells you it was real. You can only deny it if you deliberately try to deny it.

"The world is here, and I think we just have to accept that. You can argue it all you want, but I can still pick up a stick and snap it in your face, and that will wipe out all your arguments.

"We have to face it. The world is here, and it got here because God put it here. Without God, there is no world. That much I'm prepared to believe. The world remains where it is because God wills it so. In a sense, we are all just parts of God's will. Maybe we *are* part of a dream, but it's God's dream. And God's dream is what we call reality."

Scott just stared at John for a moment. Then he spoke. "Man, I think I need a drink."

"Oh now, don't get me started on that topic. If you think you're getting a sermon now, you don't know what you'd be in for! A little hellfire and brimstone."

"No, I don't really want one," Scott said. "It's just that all this talk about God and the universe and dreams . . . it's confusing. I never thought about it before, and there's so much to think about. Like OK, we exist. I never really doubted that anyway. I just wanted to see how you'd answer it. *I* know I exist. That's one thing I know, at least. But *why* do I exist? What's my purpose in the universe? And damn it, what am I supposed to do? Just answer that one question for me, because that's the one that's making me crazy. What the hell am I supposed to do?"

"Your problem—and it's a problem so many people have—is that you don't understand your own nature as a human being. I've seen this again and again in my life.

So much unhappiness, so much emptiness in people. And I've known many successful people, many famous people, as well as many poor, struggling people, but it's the same everywhere. People like you and me, we're a lost generation. We've lost touch with our true selves.

"As human beings, we're in a halfway situation. Part of us is divine, because we come from God. We all have God in us. Yet part of us is human. And as humans, we make mistakes, we do wrong. We're all sinners, all of us. Some worse than others, sure, but none of us is really able to throw the first stone. It's our two-sided nature that causes this.

"We have two parts: body and soul. Our body belongs to the earth, to physical things. Our souls belong to the other world, the spiritual realm. It's our bodies that make us fail. It's our bodies that are weak."

"The sins of the flesh," Scott said. "I know all about those."

"Exactly," John continued. "The sins of the flesh are what do us in. That's where we get tempted to go wrong. But it's so important to keep our bodies clean because the soul can't survive in a dirty temple. I believe that our souls can die if we turn to evil, if we mistreat and abuse our bodies. And there are many ways to do that. Not just physical abuse, but mental abuse, being evil, committing sin. That's all abusing your body. You can't abuse your soul because that remains pure, above and beyond life on this earth. But as long as we're alive, the soul needs the body to survive. After we die, our souls can leave us and go on. But only if they are still healthy. I think many people die physically in such a state that their souls are dead or dying. Then they don't go on. That's the only true death."

"That's fascinating," Scott said. "I've never heard that before. I've never heard it explained quite that way. It makes a lot of sense."

"It does. That's why it's so important to be good, to avoid sinfulness and wickedness. It all takes it toll on your physical side. And then when the physical side gives out, you may find that your soul is too weak to make the journey to the other realm, and it will just wither and die.''

"But what about being good? I mean, how do we know what's good and what's evil? Nobody seems to be able to make up their minds about anything these days. There's so much controversy over things, like abortion or homosexuals or sex education. How can we tell what's right and wrong anymore? It seems like everything's right and everything's wrong. It just depends on who you're asking.''

"That's very true.''

John shook his head a bit. He looked as if the idea made him very sad.

"It's one of the great diseases of modern life,'' John continued. "This idea that anything is good or bad depending on who you're asking. It wasn't always like that. I remember when I was growing up. I was as poor as could be. We had next to nothing, really, but we knew what was right and what was wrong. We might not always have abided by the rules, mind you, but everybody knew what the rules were. There wasn't a moment's hesitation about that.

"Now it's all changed. I see it in the young people today. They're lost. They're just drifting along, like they were on a raft at sea. They have no idea that the waves are getting higher and higher around them. Then all of a sudden, they get swamped. The raft gets knocked over and they fall into the sea and drown. And they never know it's coming. I've seen so much of that. I've seen so many lives wasted, so many good people fall to ruin because they had no control over the things around them, because they couldn't tell right from wrong.''

"Somebody's got to know. Don't you think somebody's got to know? I mean, only one side of an issue can be right, right? Can two opposite things both be right at the same time?''

"It doesn't seem logical, but if you look at the world, it's obvious that different people believe different things."

"Sure, but some of them must be wrong. And how can you tell? How do I know what's right and what isn't?"

"You have to get down to basics again, Scott. Before you can tell what's good or what's evil, you need to understand what good and evil are.

"The universe is a creation of God, like I've said, and that means it's good. How could it be otherwise? If God is good, He would have made a good universe. But surely there's bad in the world, and plenty of it. How do you account for that? How do you explain the bad in the world if God is good?"

"No way, now you're getting way over my head. I don't understand any of that. To me, it doesn't make sense. I would answer that you're wrong to begin with, that God isn't good, or he isn't there at all, and that the universe isn't good either. I know that goes against what you said, but it's the only answer that makes sense to me. There's too much bad to see things any other way."

"You've come up against one of life's great questions," John said. "It's the biggest question we have about God. Why did He allow evil to exist? Couldn't He just have made a perfect world, where we'd all be at peace and living in happiness? Well, think about it a moment, Scott. Can you think of any reason why we need evil, why it's necessary?"

"Yeah. It keeps lawyers in business, like my wife."

"Maybe if God is a lawyer, that could be. But think of this. If you put your hand over an open fire, how do you know it's hot?"

"It burns. What else? I can feel that it's hot."

"OK, but how do you know what you're feeling is heat? How do you know it's not cold? Or in between?"

"Because I know what cold feels like, and I know that hot feels different than cold."

"Now you're getting there. Think a little more. What

has to exist for you to know something is hot? What else has to exist?''

"Cold, I guess."

"Exactly. If there were no cold, there could be no hot. Each one is defined by the other. What is cold? It's not hot. What's hot? It's something that's not cold. See? One can't exist without the other.''

"And that applies to good and bad?''

"It does. God had to create evil at the moment He created good because if there was no evil, there could be no good. One is needed for the other. You can't feel happy if you don't know what it's like to feel sad. You can't feel warm and safe if you don't know what it's like to feel cold and insecure. Everything depends on its opposite.''

"So we have to have bad to understand good. That makes sense. But does there have to be so much bad? Couldn't we have understood it without it getting so out of hand?''

"That's our fault, though. Humans are the ones who let so much bad exist. But really, I'm not so sure there is such a thing as evil. There might not be.''

"But you just finished explaining how you can't have one without the other. Now you're saying there's no such thing as evil?''

"Let me try to be clearer here. It's like this. Good is like a light. It shines and brings warmth and makes all life possible. Without light, we couldn't live. Evil is a lack of light, a darkness. So there's really no such thing as evil, in itself. Evil is just a lack of light.''

"I don't get it. What's the difference? You sound like you're just playing with words.''

"Maybe I am, Scott, maybe I am. I'm not so sure about this myself. But let me try to explain it using an example.

"Let's say you had a doughnut.''

"A doughnut? You've gotta be kidding.''

"No really!'' John laughed at himself. "A doughnut.''

"What kind of doughnut? Chocolate? Jelly?''

"I don't know what kind! Whatever kind you like!"

"No, you have to tell me what kind or I don't want to hear this. It won't work if I don't know what kind."

"Are you always this difficult?"

"Usually, yeah."

"Lord, no wonder your wife divorced you!"

"Hey, low blow, John!"

"Yeah, I take it back. I didn't mean that."

"Besides, doughnuts had nothing to do with our divorce."

"I hope not. But can I get on with this now?"

"No, not until you tell me what kind of doughnut."

"Oh for heaven's sake, all right. A glazed doughnut, OK. A regular, glazed doughnut."

"I don't like glazed, make it chocolate."

John picked up a stick and shook it at Scott.

"I'll give you doughnuts, you young punk! OK, OK, whatever you like. A chocolate doughnut. Fine! Now what the heck was I saying?"

Both men laughed at this.

"You were telling me something about good and bad. Then you had to mention a doughnut for some stupid reason."

"That's it!" John said. "Now I remember. And listen, it's not that stupid. Maybe it's not the greatest example in the world, but it gets my point across. Now shut up and listen!

"I was saying how evil is a lack of good, right?"

"Yeah, I remember that part."

"So now let's say you had a doughnut. Don't say anything! I'll hit you with that stick if you do!

"Now, a doughnut has a hole in the middle, right? Everybody knows that. Even a chocolate doughnut has a hole in the middle. But what's a hole?"

"Oh boy, here we go again!"

"No, really! Answer it, if you're so smart. What's a

hole? Can you show me a hole? Can you hold one in your hand?''

"No, I can't hold one, but I can dig one for you. I can show you a hole in the ground."

"But all you're showing me is a space where there's no dirt. You're still not showing me the hole."

"Ah c'mon, this is silly."

"No, listen to me. It's not silly. It's an important distinction. There's really no such thing as a hole. A hole is just a place where something isn't. There's no doughnut in the middle of the doughnut, so we call it a hole. If you dig a hole, you're just making a space where there's no dirt. So we call it a hole. But there's no hole!''

"I don't know about this."

"Then if you don't believe it, go and get me a hole. Go on, pick one up. Show it to me. You can show me a doughnut. You can show me the ground around the hole. You can pick up the doughnut and you can pick up the dirt. But you can't pick up the hole, because there isn't any hole to pick up. It doesn't exist."

"All right. What the hell. I guess that makes sense. I just wish I had a chocolate doughnut now."

"See, and it makes sense when you talk about good and bad. Good is like that chocolate doughnut of yours. You can see the good. But the bad is when you eat up all the doughnut and there's nothing left but the hole. See, when all the good is gone there's nothing left but the bad. But still, the bad doesn't exist, it has no life of its own."

"It seems crazy, but it makes some kind of sense to me."

"I'm glad," John said. "But you have to use that knowledge, make it work for you."

"And how do I do that?"

"Remember what I said at the start. Good is like light, and bad is the lack of light, or the darkness. What we have to do with our lives is to seek out the light, to seek out the good and to shun the darkness, to move away from it as much as possible. It's always going to be there, because without darkness we can't have light, but you have to stay away from it. Too many people move into the darkness and stay there. They enjoy it there. In a lot of ways, the dark side of life is more comfortable, it's easier, it's more fun. But in the end, you just end up cold and blind and dead in the dark. It doesn't lead anywhere because when it's dark, you can't see where you're going.''

"That was my life, John. That was it exactly. I was just walking in the dark. It *was* fun and comfortable like you said. It really had me fooled for a long time. But you can only walk around in the dark for so long. Sooner or later you're bound to bump into something, to fall over something and get hurt.''

"And that's what happened to you, Scott. It happens to many people. There was a time in my life when I was deep in the dark. I was so far in I couldn't see the way out anymore.''

"How did you get out?''

"I made the decision to follow the light. It took a long time to find it. My life had grown so dark that there was no light left to follow. I stumbled around for a time more, but then one day it was there. It was a dim light, dim and far away, but once I was focused on it, once I knew the direction to take, I knew I could save myself. And I did. I kept going after it and going after it. Sometimes you get a little setback, and the darkness grows heavier around you. But if you keep your eyes focused on the light all the time, it won't fail you. You can't turn your eyes because you'll lose sight of it, and you might never find it again. But the light won't fail you. The light will stay true. The rest is up to you.''

"Yeah, but so much stuff gets in the way. So much stuff blocks out the light all the time.''

"Nobody said it was easy, Scott. I said that in the beginning. There's a lot of pain involved. And the world will throw all sorts of stuff in your way, all sorts of distractions and temptations to stray from the path. A lot of people lose their way and never find the light. But you have to believe in its power, you have to believe in yourself. Believe you can make it.''

"But do we really have that kind of strength? Sometimes I think I have no control over anything, that I'm just a victim of fate. No matter what I do, things are going to turn out however they are meant to turn out. What could I have done about my marriage? It just happened to me. They say we have free will, but do we really? Do we really have control over things?''

"You know how to ask the big questions, Scott, you surely do.''

"But I'm looking to you for the big answers, John. You've given me an awful lot to think about already. A lot of good sense. But what about this one? You had your problems. Were they anything you could have stopped?''

"Answer this for me, Scott. Be honest. Do you *feel* free? Or do you feel like you're under control?''

"Well . . .'' Scott hesitated.

"Be honest now. Say what you really feel.''

"Well, I guess I do feel free, if you ask me straight out like that. I could get up now if I wanted and walk away from you. Or I could stay here. Or I could go to sleep. I suppose I can do whatever I want. So I guess I'm free. But that's because I'm up here in the mountains. It's not so easy back in the real world. There are so many pressures on you, so many influences. I don't think I'm so free there.''

"That's true enough. There are forces in the world, powers we can't understand. And they have an impact on our lives. They push you and pull you and you don't even know it. You think certain things and you don't know why. You get ideas but you don't know where they come from. They're just there all of a sudden. There's a lot more out there than we're aware of. More than we understand. And you can't measure the impact they have on you.

"There are also more obvious temptations, things that have power over you. Temptations of the flesh, mostly. Sex, alcohol, drugs, all sorts of vices. They pull at you as well. Temptation is everywhere. How free can you be in the face of it all?"

"That's what I'm saying. How much of my life is my own? How much can I be blamed for if there are all these forces and temptations pulling at me?"

"But that's where you fall into the trap," John said. "That's the trap of no responsibility, of avoiding the blame.

"Answer this. If there are so many things shaping your life, things you can't control, things you can't resist, why do people act in different ways? Why does one man leave his wife and children when things get tough, and another man sticks by them? Wouldn't both men like to escape their troubles and run away? Why don't they all? Isn't the temptation the same for each man?

"Why does one woman turn to drink when she's troubled? Or to drugs? Most people are troubled to some degree, some terribly so. Why don't they all give in to the temptation? They know it's there. There isn't anybody these days who doesn't know that getting drunk or taking some pills could make them feel better, at least for the moment. But they don't all give in. Why is that?"

"I guess some people are stronger than others."

"Precisely. It's a matter of willpower. Everyone can be strong, but some people are too lazy. They won't make the effort. They give in to pressures, they let the world take them over. But the point is, they have the freedom to resist. They could fight it if they chose to do so. Trouble is, once you start giving in, it gets harder and harder to resist. The more you fall into darkness, the harder it is to find the light. That first step into the dark is often fatal. It's the end for a lot of people.

"There are other forces too. I believe there are ancestral forces at work in the world. No death is final. When a person dies, a little bit of them lives on and stays here on earth. Over the years, these powers—call them spirits, or ghosts, whatever you like—these powers exert an influence on us that we aren't aware of. The world is full of spirits.

"Sometimes we're born with another spirit inside of us. It lives within us and it influences our behavior without our knowing it. It could be a good spirit or a bad one. But it's there. Different places have spirits too. Some places are good. Some places, I think, are just evil. Not like in a horror movie, where the ghosts come out and try to kill you. It's a much quieter influence. It's deep in your mind, in a place you can't get at. But it's there. It's there all the time."

"You think so? You really think we can live forever that way?"

"Well, that's just a part of it. It's like an essence, a remnant of you that lives on. Your soul goes on to a different world, a different level of life. Maybe the level where God is, where there's no more time to worry about.

"We're all a part of God, and God is eternal. So how could we be anything but eternal ourselves?

"This is something I think you can sense. You can just feel it if you open yourself up to it. You can sense your immortality. You can see it around you, in the face of a newborn baby, in the beauty of these mountains, in the power of the oceans. How could all that wonder just stop when you die? How could it all be for no reason? If we just die when we die, what's the point of God's glorious creation? It would all be a waste of time. It would be stupid. And I certainly don't think God would waste His time with stupid behavior. He left that for us."

"So we will live on?"

"Yes, we'll live on, but only if we keep our souls alive. Like I was saying before, life on earth is a trial for us. It's the one chance we get to make sure our souls will live on. It's God's test for us, to see if we measure up. If we don't, if we fall into the darkness, our souls will die, and we'll disappear.

"But if we keep to the light, if we stay on the right path, our souls will live, and they'll pass on to the next world. The world where we can finally be at peace."

"Keep to the light." Scott quietly said the words to himself. Then he looked toward the horizon.

"Look!" Scott said. "The light!"

The first fragment of dawn was making itself seen. A line was drawn between the darkness of sky and earth, and the two separated, signaling the birth of a new day.

"Morning in the mountains is always a beautiful sight," John said. "But I think it's time we got a little sleep. What do you say?"

"Sleep? I hope I can sleep, with all that you've given me to think about. A lot of it is still unclear to me. But you know what?"

"What, Scott?"

"I think I can see the light now. I think I know which way to go."

John smiled at him.

"Time for some sleep, my friend. Time for some sleep."

Scott lay down, facing the dawn. Thoughts were racing through his head. But the night had taken its toll. Before long, he was sound asleep. He slept long and peacefully. He hadn't slept so well in years.

When he woke up in the early afternoon, John was gone. Scott looked all over for him, calling out his name. He couldn't believe John had gone. He wanted to ask him more questions, to find out more about what he knew. He was so wise, this stranger in the woods. He knew so many answers to the questions Scott had. Disappointed and sad, Scott sat down to collect himself. Then he noticed a note tucked under his backpack.

He opened it up.

Dear Scott,

I'm sorry to walk out on you this way, but I feel it's better. You see, my name isn't John Burrows. It's something else. I'd like to tell you, but I have to keep it a secret. It's for your own protection as well as mine.

I would have liked to talk with you more, but I think you're on the right path now. I think things are going to work out for you.

I hope someday we can meet again, in more favorable circumstances. I think that day may come in the future, but not quite yet.

I wish you all the best, in your long struggle toward the light. It won't be easy. There will be more pain ahead for you. But now you know what you have to do.

God bless you my friend. And keep on toward the light.

The letter was not signed.

Scott packed up his things and hit the trail again. He made it to Mt. Mitchell that evening. As he stood there watching the sun go down, thinking about John Burrows, the wise man on the trail, and the things he had said, Scott knew that the setting sun was a symbol of his own life. One part of his life had ended there in the mountains. A new chapter was starting. It would all begin again for him. As the sun would rise again the next morning, Scott would rise with it, ready to follow the light wherever it led him, knowing always that the light could lead only to good.

He turned his back on the setting sun, just as he turned his back on the darkness. He lay down again, still tired from the previous night, but with a clear head. He never turned around to see the sun again, even though the sunset was beautiful. He was through with watching the darkness fall. He wanted to get to sleep early, so he could wake up in time to see the sunrise. That's what interested him now. The sunrise.

He was asleep before the first stars appeared.

* * *

It was not until months later that Scott saw a television show about Elvis Presley in which he learned that "John Burrows" was a common alias Presley used. That's when he made the connection. The man on the trail was indeed Elvis Presley. But he wasn't the famous Elvis Presley anymore. Now he was just like Scott. Another unknown person, another person stumbling his way toward the light.

A SECOND DEATH?

While there have been hundreds of reports that Elvis did not die on August 16, 1977, few people are aware of a man named Jaimie C., who claims Elvis in fact died on January 2, 1989.

Jaimie, like many others, insists the "death" in 1977 was faked. Elvis wanted to escape from the turmoil of his life to live in peace. To do so he moved to a place where he was far less likely to be bothered: South America.

It is unclear where in South America Elvis was purportedly living, though it would seem to have been in the central region of the continent, probably toward the western side. This would most likely place him in Bolivia or Argentina, but Paraguay, northern Chile, and southern Peru cannot be ruled out.

In any event, if the story is true, the location is immaterial, because Elvis did not survive the harrowing events of this tale. Here, then, is a retelling of what might be called "The Second Death of Elvis Presley."

* * *

The weather forecasts weren't favorable, but Elvis wanted to go. Jaimie C., his longtime friend, warned him against it, but he knew that when Elvis made up his mind it was hard to change it.

It is unclear why they were flying, but this much is certain: they would be traveling in a small plane over a harsh, mountainous region. Even in good weather, the winds could be strong and unpredictable. Flying in bad weather was asking for trouble.

They would be flying over a stretch of the great Andes Mountains in Bolivia. There are two main mountain chains, or *cordilleras,* in Bolivia, known as the Western and Eastern Cordillera, respectively. It is here that the Andes Mountains reach their widest point, stretching over four hundred miles across. In the Western Cordillera the peaks range from eighteen thousand feet to over twenty-one thousand feet. In the Eastern Cordillera the mountains are equally high, dominated by two giant peaks, Illampu (20,873 ft.) and Illimani (21,201 ft.). By any measure, these are among the most formidable mountain ranges in the world and a death trap for any small plane that might find itself in trouble.

It would be the pilot's task to traverse the Eastern Cordillera. The flight seems to have been headed for Bolivia's largest city, La Paz, located high in the Andes in the region called the Altiplano, a wide plateau that separates the two mountain chains. The pilot, who knew that the weather reports indicated trouble, was very hesitant to go. But most people in Bolivia are poor, and the pilot had many relatives depending on him. This was a well-paying job, particularly by Bolivian standards. He didn't want to risk being fired. After all, if the rich American wanted to go now, he would go now, and if one pilot wouldn't take him, he could find another who would. The lure of the money was too great to resist. So saying a prayer to the Virgin Mary and his patron saints to protect him, the pilot fired up the plane and prepared himself for the worst. With God's help, at least, he might make it.

A Second Death?

Jaimie tried one last time to convince Elvis to put off the journey or to travel by some other means. But Elvis insisted he had to go.

The weather was clear as the plane took off, but weather changes quickly in the mountains, and Jaimie and the pilot both feared what lay ahead.

For the first hour or so everything went well. They had crossed over the beginning of the Cordillera, and the sky was still clear. The pilot (we will call him Simon) thought the saints were with him and he started to feel more at ease. Weather was always hard to predict in the mountains. Perhaps the reports were incorrect. Simon soon learned that they weren't, though whether or not the saints were with him remains to be seen.

As Simon scanned the sky, a thin black line appeared on the horizon. It seemed to have no end, stretching right and left as far as he could see. There was no chance of circumventing it.

The clouds rose up quickly. Within ten minutes the sky was thick with the ominous, black shroud. Elvis and Jaimie were in the back of the plane, still unaware of what was approaching. Simon quietly called to Jaimie.

Jaimie headed to the front. Elvis was asleep in the rear of the plane. Jaimie had been lying in the darkened cabin, wondering about what would happen. Now he saw it.

"Madre de Dios," he said, when he saw the storm. "Mother of God." It was surely a call for help.

"What can we do?" he said to Simon. "Can't we turn around and go back?"

"Not anymore," Simon said, with fear in his voice. "The storm is coming too quickly. It would overtake us. Then we would be riding along with it and never get out of it. The only hope is to pass through it. We must pray that while the storm is wide, it may not be too deep."

"And if it is?"

"If it is? If it is, we are all dead." Simon spoke with the blunt honesty of a man who has lived with death all

131

his life. He was afraid, certainly. Only a crazy man would not be. But he would not let his fear overwhelm him. If he had to face this storm, he would face it. He would do what he could to save his own life and the lives of the others. Simon was a skilled pilot and had maneuvered through storms before. But this one was different. This one was the grandmother of all storms.

Though the clouds were still distant, Jaimie and Simon now began to feel the wind. The flight turned bumpy as powerful gusts swatted at the plane, trying to knock it backward. Simon took the plane lower, trying to avoid the worst of the storm. Were he in a powerful jet aircraft, he might be able to rise above it. But in his small plane the only hope was to get down under it and hope the worst was up above.

That might not be the case, but at least it offered something other than certain destruction. And if circumstances grew desperate, a tiny chance existed that he could land the plane in the mountains. The odds of finding a landing site were almost nil, but Simon had the hope that all religious men have, the hope that an unseen hand would guide him to a safe destination.

The ride grew worse and worse. The wind howled outside the plane. The clouds reared up in front of them, a glowering, incomprehensible, natural force. There was a terrible beauty to them, as in all boundless, fundamental powers. For Simon, the storm was a manifestation of the rage of God, a sign from heaven that humanity must never consider itself too highly, never feel it can know everything or do everything. No matter what man might accomplish, God could destroy his paltry creations in an instant with one sweep of His dreaded hand.

So deeply did Simon see God in these clouds, that an unexpected peace came upon him. If he were going to die in this storm, he thought, he would be dying in the arms of God. The same arms that smote him down would then raise him up to heaven. After all, he had been a good man all his life, good to his family and friends. What reason could God have to send him to the Devil? No, if God wanted him now, it would only be to bring him to Paradise. Let it be then, Simon said, if that is what is to be. But he also knew that God would be disappointed in him if he did not do his utmost to save the lives of the others. After all, they might not be ready for heaven. It would be sinful if he were to help send them to hell.

Whatever might happen, Simon was now ready for it. He had found his peace in this, his darkest moment.

Jaimie's religious convictions were not as strong. He had the fear of a man who doubts heaven. He feared his death, for to him it would be nothing more than death, an endless darkness, an eternity in these horrible black clouds.

Neither man thought of the third passenger as they stared in wonder at the storm. They didn't know how long Elvis had been standing behind them. It wasn't until he spoke that they noticed him.

"Gentlemen," Elvis said. "I think we ought to hold hands and pray."

Needless to say, nobody objected to this idea. Elvis was always a religious man. His famous gospel albums were just one sign of his faith. Like Simon, Elvis was now staring at the power of God.

The three of them held hands as Elvis said the prayer. He asked God to forgive them and to help them see this through. Jaimie C. emphasizes that Elvis never asked to be saved himself, but he prayed for the others to live. It was a prayer that would be answered.

The prayer was over. Now it was time to fight the storm. Simon told Jaimie and Elvis to strap themselves in. Things were about to get rough.

They hit the cloud bank. It was like driving into a wall. The plane bucked and bounced as if it had a crazed life of its own. Simon did what he could to keep it steady, but it was impossible. The winds tore at the plane. He could see nothing out the windows. Snow fell too furiously for the wipers to contend with. It streamed down the windshield, obscuring all vision. The darkness outside was impenetrable. Day turned to night in a moment, as they drove on into the heart of this furious, black beast.

The plane's instruments were all Simon had to steer by, and in these conditions they were next to useless. If they were going to hit a mountain, it would come up too quickly for him to do anything. Besides, it was enough work to keep the plane moving in one direction. Sudden maneuvers were out of the question.

Simon just flew onward, hoping he could hammer the plane out the other end of the storm before he crashed. He knew the plane was being driven downward. The altitude gauge steadily declined. He tried to force the plane up, but it wouldn't respond. He couldn't turn upward too sharply, because the wind would just flip the plane over and that would be the end of them.

He felt hopeless, but he didn't give up fighting.

Then, suddenly, they hit.

With a harsh, grating sound, the plane scraped the top of a mountain. It must have torn the wheels off. This was it. Simon could do nothing now but try to keep the plane upright so it would land on its belly. He could see the ground moving beneath him. It was a dark blur, but he had something to focus on. With luck, they might survive.

The plane hit the ground again. Simon couldn't see far, but it seemed the way was clear. *God has guided us,* he thought, as the plane ground against the earth. They had struck a rare, flat part of the mountains. But how long would it last? Would the level ground end abruptly, dropping them thousands of feet into a ravine? Or could they stop in time?

They went into a skid, spinning around. Nothing could be done now. All they had was hope as fate played its hand.

Simon held on tightly. Thoughts of his family passed

through his mind. The whole thing must have lasted only a few seconds, but with death so close, time slows down. It seemed to go on and on, the plane spinning, the storm raging.

With a crash, it stopped. The plane rammed into the mountainside. They hit sideways. The walls crumpled, glass and metal flew everywhere. Simon was able to duck his head. It saved his life. Later on, he saw that a piece of flying glass had cut off the top of his seat. Had he not ducked, his head would have gone with it.

The plane was torn in several places. Snow poured in through the breaches. Simon was unaware of what had happened to Elvis and Jaimie. With the plane's lights out, he couldn't see into the back. He didn't know if they were alive or dead.

He grabbed the flashlight that was hooked under the instrument panel. It was a powerful light, and with it he made his way to the back of the plane. Traveling was difficult because the plane lay at a sharp angle and the snow entering made the floor slick. But by planning his steps carefully, Simon made it to the back.

First he came across Jaimie. He was stunned, but he seemed to be breathing. Simon felt that he would be alright. But what about Elvis?

Simon couldn't find him at first. *Didn't he strap himself in?* was the first thought that crossed his mind. *If not, he may have been thrown from the plane.* He shone his light to where he thought Elvis was sitting. There was his answer. The seat was gone.

The plane had broken right where Elvis's seat connected to the floor. The seat had been torn free by the impact. It could be anywhere, but it could also still be inside the plane.

Simon turned his light to the far rear. There he saw Elvis, his seat smashed up against the back of the plane. Was he alive?

Simon was about the make the tricky journey to the rear when he heard Jaimie call to him.

He quickly apprised Jaimie of the situation. He said he would now go see to Elvis, but Jaimie held him back.

"No," Jaimie said, "You stay here and shine the light for me. I'll go."

Simon knew that Elvis was Jaimie's friend. It was his right to go.

Jaimie made it to the rear, but it was too late. Elvis slumped in his seat, his head dangling loosely to one side. Jaimie was not certain, but he thinks Elvis's neck broke when the seat slammed into the wall. For several minutes he stayed with Elvis, crying for his dead friend. But he knew there was work to be done. He and Simon had to survive, for Elvis's sake.

Their first task was to provide themselves better shelter to weather the storm. The rear of the plane was not as sharply angled as the front. It twisted in the center, making the back half the logical place to stay. There were some heavy plastic sheets on board, and Simon and Jaimie strung these across the openings, cutting off the snow. They had a small supply of food and water, and several blankets. Now there was nothing to do but wrap themselves up, try to keep warm, and wait for the storm to end.

It didn't take long. It turned out the storm was not very deep. Perhaps a few more miles of flight would have got them through it safely. But this was speculation for another time.

The changeover was shocking. It seemed like nighttime while the storm raged. But within a matter of minutes, the storm passed and the sun shone down upon them. It wasn't even very cold anymore, once the trailing winds died down. Luck was with them again. They had been lucky in so many things, but luck was not with them all.

Their dilemma was obvious. How to get back to safety? They couldn't even be sure where they were. It might be one hundred miles away from the nearest person, or somebody could be right outside the plane.

They saw nothing when they left the plane, just mountains stretching in all directions. Simon said he would check the radio. If that worked, they shouldn't have much difficulty. Their luck held. The radio was working. Now it was a matter of contacting somebody.

Simon would work on that, but Jaimie had something else to do. He had to bury his friend.

There was no way they could get Elvis down from here, he decided. It would be better to let him rest in peace. He scouted around for a while and found the perfect location. There was a rock formation that formed a natural tomb. It was long and deep, open only on one end. The body could be placed in this hole and the entrance easily covered. This would be the place.

Simon and Jaimie carried Elvis's body to the rocks. They placed him inside. Together, they prayed over the dead King's form. Slowly, with great sorrow, Jaimie covered the makeshift tomb, and the King was sealed away forever in this grave on the top of the world.

The pain was too much for Jaimie to bear. He climbed to the top of the rocks that held Elvis, and with all his might he cried out, a helpless wail of pain at this loss, this second death, this real death. The scream echoed and reechoed in the mountains.

It was not long afterward that they heard voices. At first, they thought the shock had affected them, but the voices grew louder and louder. Then they saw people. It was a group of Indians. There were still people living in these rugged mountains. It seems they were nearby and had heard Jaimie's cry.

This, for most purposes, is the end of the tale. The Indians were able to lead Jaimie and Simon to safety. Simon and Jaimie spoke at length on their journey back to civilization, and this is how we know of Simon's thoughts and what he did during the crash. The two men parted then. Simon went back to his life. Jaimie has never seen him again.

Jaimie survived to tell his tale. He insists it is true. He insists that Elvis lies somewhere in the Eastern Cordillera, under the rocks, among the clouds.

Postscript: There is no way to verify this story, other than through an extensive expedition into the Andes Mountains. However, in the interest of accuracy, we must mention the following. This story is known to us only through Jaimie C. And while he claims the events told here occurred on January 2, 1989, there have been numerous sightings of Elvis since that time. This would seem to disprove Jaimie's account. Nevertheless, it is an intriguing tale, another piece of the mystery that Elvis Presley has become.

GOING FISHIN'

It was a fine day for playing hooky, and that was enough for Clyde and James. Of course, you couldn't really call it hooky, since they were taking days off from work that were due to them, but it was more fun to look at it that way. What it meant was getting away from the heavy lifting at the agricultural supplier and heading off to their favorite bass lake for the day. It was the summer of 1984.

It was a small lake in one of the less-traveled parts of Georgia. The bass there weren't the biggest and the fishing wasn't the best, but most of the time they could have the lake to themselves if they went on a weekday. And it wasn't the fish that interested them so much. What they really liked was sitting back, drinking some beers, putting away the big basket of food they brought, and just shooting the breeze. There were few friends closer than Clyde and James, and they could spend a whole day talking about nothing.

They had spent the morning slowly moving from one spot to another, making lazy casts and catching a few small ones. The sun was hot, the sky was clear, a light breeze was blowing to keep it comfortable; it was a perfect day. They never suspected what was about to happen.

"Shoot!" Clyde said suddenly, "Look over there."

He pointed out toward the center of the lake. James turned to see another boat heading their way.

"Well I'll be damned," James said. "Clyde, I thought you reserved this lake for us!"

Both of them hated it when another boat appeared, something which rarely happened, though there was no reason to be bothered. Fishermen always respected each other's territory, and an intruding boat never came very close. But there was something about being alone on a lake that Clyde and James loved, and even one small boat way on the other side would diminish their enjoyment.

But this time things were even worse.

"What the hell's that fool doing?" James said, as the boat came closer and closer. "He'll scare hell out of the fish!"

James didn't care about the fish, but he surely didn't like another boat bearing down on them that way.

"Damned nerve," Clyde muttered. "Got a lot a damn nerve moving in on us like that."

The boat just kept coming. It was a large boat for that small lake, with a lot more engine power than was necessary. It moved slowly but steadily toward them. They could make out three men and a woman on board. Two of the men were dressed oddly for a fishing trip. They wore shirts and ties, and they must've been baking in the heat.

The other man was dressed casually, with jeans and a blue pocket T-shirt. What caught their eye most, however, was the woman. She was a knockout, tall and shapely with long, blond hair. She wore a halter top and cutoff jeans that showed off the best pair of legs they'd ever seen. She sat high up in one of the fishing seats, giving the two men a great view.

"Well, look at that," James said. "Clyde, why'd you

want that boat to stay away? Shoot, I hope they ram right into us now!"

The boat cut its engines and pulled up to within fifteen feet of Clyde and James. The man in jeans, who seemed to be the only one with a fishing rod near him, called out to the two friends.

"Hey, fellas, any luck today?"

"Just a couple of small ones," Clyde said. "But then again we're not trying very hard."

"Well, I'm not too familiar with these waters," the man said. "I was hoping you could direct me to one of the better spots."

"Aren't any better spots," James replied. "You want to catch some big bass you'd best go someplace else. I can tell you where you can catch a lot, but don't expect any size."

"That would be fine," the man said.

James told him about two different areas that usually produced a lot of bass if you fished them right. The three of them then fell into a casual conversation about what lures to use and how to present them, just typical fisherman chatter.

Meanwhile, the two men with ties seemed very nervous. They kept looking around impatiently, as if they couldn't wait to leave. The beautiful woman seemed bored. She flipped through a magazine without much interest. Clyde and James tried not to be too obvious about looking at her, but they'd never before seen a woman so beautiful, and it was hard not to stare.

The whole time this was going on, Clyde had a funny feeling. The man in jeans looked too familiar. It dawned on him that he resembled Elvis Presley, but of course that was ridiculous. Must be a coincidence. Maybe he was one of those Elvis impersonators. A showbiz guy: that would explain the beautiful, bored woman and the men in ties. They could be a couple of agents or producers, city guys who probably hated fishing more than anything.

Just to be safe, Clyde thought he'd introduce himself.

"We haven't really introduced ourselves," he said. "My name is Clyde. This is my buddy James. We're just running away from work today to have a little relaxation."

"I'm running away too," the Elvis look-alike said. When he said this, the men in ties nearly jumped into the air. They looked horrified. Clyde wondered more and more.

"My name's John," Elvis said. "Johnny Burroughs. Glad to know you."

Clyde wondered about the name. He didn't expect Elvis would admit who he was, yet the name "John Burroughs" faintly rang a bell. Where had Clyde heard it before?

They chatted a little more about fishing, until James thought he'd be friendly and offer John a beer. He held out a can of Budweiser, but John declined.

"I'm not much of a drinker," he said. "And we've got some beer on board I really don't need. You're welcome to it."

Burroughs then said something to one of the other men. The man reluctantly went below deck and came back with a cooler.

"Come on over," Burroughs said.

Clyde maneuvered his boat next to the larger vessel, and the man who had got the cooler lowered it to James.

"I'll just take a couple and give it back," James said, "We've got plenty as it is."

"No, no now," Burroughs said, "Keep the whole thing. The whole cooler. Really, I appreciate all your advice and I'd like to show my appreciation someway. Believe me, it's nothing."

"Well, alright," James said. "Hell, a man offers me a cooler full of beer I'm not gonna try too hard to have him change his mind."

Clyde had moved his boat a bit away again, to avoid bumping, when one of the nervous men said, "We better move along, John. We shouldn't stay too long."

John looked pretty peeved at this, and he snapped at that man.

"Dammit!" he said, "I'm tired of you always trying to take me away from a good time! I'm not done talking yet, now leave me be."

The nervous men were almost shaking. The beautiful woman just shook her head and laughed a little.

Then she got an idea.

"Hey, John," she said, with a mischievous look in her eye, "why don't you sing something for us."

One of the nervous men flipped at her remark.

"Dammit to hell, why don't you mind your business!" he shouted. "Don't make any fool suggestions like that!"

Burroughs quickly turned on him.

"Don't you speak to her that way! You seem to forget too often who's in charge here. I think that sounds like a damn good idea."

Burroughs then turned to Clyde and James.

"You fellas mind a little song?"

"Not at all," Clyde said. "Maybe you can sing one to the fish, try to make 'em bite."

Clyde was trying to be casual, but he was really beginning to think this could be Elvis Presley. Everything pointed that way. But how could it be? Elvis was dead!

Burroughs had picked up a guitar that was lying on deck. He strapped it on. Then he laughed a little and said, half to himself, "Sing one to the fish. I think I'll try that."

He started to play an old, talking blues riff. He just played for a few verses, as if he were trying to remember the words. Then he started singing the craziest song Clyde and James had ever heard in their lives. They couldn't remember it all later on, but a few lines stuck in their minds. It went something like this:

> *Been sittin' on a lake,*
> *Been lookin' for bass,*
> *While Eddie and Bob*

Are a pain in the ass!
Yeah I'm a fishing man,
Just a fishing man,
Working on my tan,
And I don't give a damn.

The song went on for a few more improvised verses. Most of it didn't make any sense to Clyde and James. Obviously, John Burroughs was singing about people and things they knew nothing about. While he did, the beautiful woman would break out into hysterical laughter. She certainly knew what the song was about. Eddie and Bob, who seemed to be the men with ties, just stomped off to the back of the boat muttering to themselves.

While this was going on, Clyde nearly went into shock. He realized it for sure now. The singing voice was unmistakable. It was the voice of Elvis Presley.

When the song was over, Burroughs laughed loud and long with the beautiful woman. Clyde just stared with his mouth hanging open. James, who had also come to think it was Elvis, did the same.

Finally, Burroughs—or Elvis—looked toward them. Something seemed to change in his expression. He had the face of someone who had taken a joke a little too far and now realized it might get him into trouble.

He put the guitar down quickly.

"Well, I hope you liked my song," he said, somewhat nervously, to Clyde and James. "But I guess I'd better go now and let you fellas get back to your fishing."

As soon as he said this, Eddie and Bob leaped for the controls of the boat. They fired up the engine and started to turn the boat around.

Clyde, realizing he might never have the chance again, called out.

"Hey, John," he cried. "Are you Elvis Presley?"

Burroughs just smiled at him and said, "I hope you enjoy that beer. Thanks for everything."

144

He seemed about to say more when one of the other men gunned the engine. The boat took off like a shot, leaving Clyde and James behind in its huge wake. They watched it go. It didn't go to the fishing spots James had mentioned. Instead, it went all the way across to the far end of the lake. It was hard to see exactly what was happening, but it seemed that a trailer and several cars were waiting there. They did see that the boat was taken out of the water and driven away.

The whole time Clyde and James just watched. They didn't say a word.

Finally, Clyde turned to James.

"That was Elvis Presley," he said. "That was Elvis Presley."

"Elvis Presley's dead," James replied. "But I'm with you. Dead or not, that sure seemed to be him."

They couldn't imagine who else it could be.

The rest of the day was spent reliving the whole strange event: the large, overly powerful boat; the suspicious men wearing shirts and ties for a fishing trip; the beautiful woman; the strange song; and the great singing voice.

It might have been an impersonator, they figured, but they didn't think an impersonator would have the money for a boat like that, and he wouldn't need to have those men with him. Why would Eddie and Bob be so anxious to leave if it were just an impersonator? Why did Burroughs, or Elvis, make those remarks about running away? Why did his mood suddenly seem to change? And why didn't he ever go fishing after that?

It didn't make any sense. If it wasn't Elvis, there would have been no need to run away. But Clyde and James couldn't get over the fact that Elvis was supposed to be dead. It wasn't until four years later, when stories about Elvis's being alive began to appear, that Clyde and James realized that the man on the lake might very well have been Elvis Presley.

Clyde and James still play hooky whenever they get an

opportunity. And they still don't like it when another boat shows up on their lake. But there's one boat they keep looking for. And ever since that day, they never go out on the lake without a camera. Because next time they get a chance to land a big one, they won't let it get away.

MORE SHORT SIGHTINGS

Belinda R. was out shopping for shoes for her kids, eight-year-old Todd and six-year-old Amy. She was walking down the main street of a Florida town, heading toward an ice-cream parlor. They were going to have a treat now that the headache of shoe buying had been completed.

The kids got their ice-cream cones and the three of them were heading back to their car. Todd was acting rambunctious, teasing Amy and threatening to eat her ice cream. Belinda was telling him to knock it off when he went a bit too far and knocked into Amy, sending the top scoop of her ice-cream cone falling to the floor. On the way down, it bounced off her new white pants, leaving a large, messy, chocolate stain.

"Oh, Todd, look what you did!" Belinda yelled.

Amy started to cry about her ice cream. Belinda was more concerned about doing something about that stain. She didn't want to see those new pants ruined.

She had some napkins in her purse, and she bent down

to wipe off the stain. There was a public drinking fountain across the street. She turned to Todd.

"Todd, take this napkin and wet it in that fountain across the street. Hurry up, I want to get this stain."

"OK, Mom," he replied.

He started to go, then he stopped.

"Todd, what are you waiting for?" Belinda chided him. She had her back to him while she was busy with Amy's pants.

"Mom!" Todd said excitedly. "I see Elvis Presley!"

"Sure you do, Todd." Belinda was too perturbed to play any of Todd's games. "That's great. Now go get that water."

"No, Mom, I mean it! He just came out of that dentist's office!"

Belinda was angry now. She turned halfway around towards Todd. "You better get across that street, young man, or you're going to need a dentist for your broken teeth! Now go!"

"But Mom, it's really him!"

"Go, I said!"

"Aww, Mom!" Todd complained, but he went, reluctantly.

He ran back across with the wet napkin. Belinda worked on the stain once again.

"Mom!"

"What is it now, Todd?"

"Elvis is still here. He's talking to a man across the street. They're standing by that big car."

"Yes, Todd, whatever you say." Belinda was having none of it.

"Mom, can I go over and ask him for his autograph?"

"No, Todd, you may not!" His mother was getting exasperated. "For God's sake, Todd, Elvis Presley is dead."

"But it's him, Mom. Just like on the covers of your record albums! Really, it's him!"

Belinda had got out about as much of the stain as she

could. She calmed down a little now, and she was feeling sorry for being so short-tempered with Todd.

She turned to him. "OK, Todd, where's Elvis?"

"It's too late! He got into the car already."

"What car?"

"That one, across the street. See? It's turning around."

The car made a three-point turn across the street. Belinda watched it turning. She didn't want Todd to feel bad, so she tried to talk him out of what he thought he saw.

"Now listen, it couldn't possibly be Elvis Presley, because he's dead, like I said. It must've been somebody who looked like him."

As she finished saying this, the car passed by. There, in the passenger seat, Belinda saw Elvis Presley.

Todd still says, "I told you so."

It was Wednesday. Like every Wednesday, Helen had visited her sister. Now she was heading home.

She drove along on a two-lane street in Dayton, Ohio. Helen took the right lane. She preferred the slower lane because at seventy-one years old her reflexes were not what they used to be. Most people drove too fast for her now, so it was not unusual when a cab passed her in the left lane. What she didn't like was the way it swerved in front of her, cutting her off.

She may have been seventy-one, but Helen had a lot of fighting spirit. She wasn't going to let him get away with it.

When the cab cut back into the left lane again, Helen decided she'd try to yell at the driver at the next light if she could catch up to him. She had to go a little faster than she was comfortable with, but when her dander was up she was a pretty tough customer.

The cab rode a little ahead of her, but it looked like she'd make it. The light ahead turned red, and there was one car in each lane ahead of them. She'd have her chance to tell that driver a thing or two.

She rolled down her window and pulled up next to the cab. She was about to call for the driver's attention when she glanced at the passenger in the back. She couldn't believe her eyes. It was Elvis Presley.

As if that weren't enough, he rolled down his window. He leaned slightly out of the window and spoke to her.

"Sorry about cutting you off like that, ma'am. You can be sure I'll take it out of his tip."

Helen was too shocked to reply. The light changed, and the cab drove off. Helen followed.

She wasn't sure what to do. Should she follow the car? What would she do if she did?

Unfortunately, her questions were answered for her. The car in front of her started to slow down. It came to a stop. Helen was so caught up in thinking about Elvis that she nearly hit the car in front of her. For some reason, the car had stalled, leaving Helen trapped behind it. She was too close to swing out into the left lane, and the cars behind her were moving over, blocking her in.

With frustration, she watched as the cab turned a corner up ahead. She finally got out of the spot she was in, but by the time she turned the same corner, the cab was long gone.

Shannon had been working at the jewelry store for only a few months, so it was not surprising that she made a mistake. Some packages had arrived by messenger. They contained some new items for sale. Normally, Shannon would open the packages and clean the pieces, making them suitable for display. What she didn't know was that all packages marked with a red X were only to be opened by the boss.

She picked up the X package like any other and began opening it. Her boss saw her and stopped her before she could see what was inside it. He realized that he had never told her that rule before, because in the short time Shannon had worked there, there had been no such packages delivered.

Shannon was curious about what it contained, but her boss took it into his private office. Having a lot of work to do, Shannon soon forgot about it. It wasn't until several hours later that she noticed her boss bringing a jewelry box out of his office. It was about the size of a necklace case, only a bit wider. Shannon thought that this had to be the mysterious delivery.

Sure enough, her boss told her that a woman would be picking the case up sometime within the hour. It was already paid for, and the woman would identify herself as "Claire." Shannon was to give the box to the woman if her boss was in his office when Claire arrived.

The boss waited around for about fifteen minutes, but he was an impatient man, and he finally wandered back into his office. This was Shannon's chance. She had to take a peek.

A little scared at the chance she was taking, she picked up the jewelry box. Looking around to see if anyone was looking, she lifted the lid and saw a strange and remarkable piece of jewelry. It was a large gold guitar, with the words "The King" imprinted on it in silver. There were some jewels on it, but the interesting thing was the great workmanship that went into the piece. It was a finely detailed work of art, complete with guitar strings and a finish that had wood grain patterns. She had never seen anything like it.

Then the front door buzzer sounded. Shannon quickly put the box back and let the customer in. A tall, beautiful woman with long brown hair entered. Shannon had never seen her before. She looked like a fashion model.

The woman came to Shannon and said her name was Claire. Shannon had guessed as much. She gave Claire the jewelry box. She took it, said thank you, and left the store.

Intrigued by the entire mystery, Shannon walked from behind the counter and looked out the window. She saw Claire getting into a large, expensive-looking car. Someone in the backseat opened the door for her. Shannon only caught a glimpse, but there was a man in the backseat who looked a lot like Elvis Presley.

Normally, Shannon wouldn't have believed it. But there was other evidence that supported what she saw.

"I think if I just saw the man in the car, I wouldn't feel the way I do," she says. "But all of it adds up.

"First, there is the package that nobody is supposed to open. Then I saw the guitar with 'The King' on it. Then this incredibly beautiful woman picks it up. What else could it all mean? Who else would have that kind of jewelry made? It must have cost a fortune."

She tried asking her boss whom the package was for. He will only say "For a rich customer." Indeed, he even claims he doesn't know who it's for. He just knows that Claire picks up the jewelry, and he always gets a bank check for payment. There is never any kind of identification on the check.

There were a few other deliveries for Claire over the next several months, but then they stopped. The boss doesn't know where Claire went, or why there are no more orders. He does know that his best customer no longer buys anything.

Shannon knows just a little bit more.

It was the busiest time of the day for Pat, who delivered food for a pizzeria. Between 4:30 and 7:30 he never had a chance to rest. Everyone was ordering dinner. He traveled from place to place as fast as he could, and as soon as he got back there were new delivereies to make. The good part was that he made a lot of money in tips over a few hours.

He didn't think anything of the order when it was given to him: five hero sandwiches delivered to a nearby motel. Just another order.

When he got there, he buzzed the room. A man came to the door and took the bag of heroes. He gave Pat a fifty-dollar bill. Pat started to make change when the man told him to keep it.

"But that's twenty-four dollars!" Pat said.

"Don't worry about it," he replied. "It's all yours."

The man started to close the door. Just before it closed, Pat believes he saw Elvis Presley walking across the room. What makes him so certain?

"Nothing, really," he says. "I did have a pretty good look at him, but it was only for a second. It looked an awful lot like him. But it was the whole feel of the situation that makes me believe it was him.

"The way the man tipped me, letting me have all that money. I think he did it because he wanted to get the door closed as quickly as possible. He didn't want to wait for me to give him the change.

"And the curtains of the room were closed. That's not unusual, but it's one more thing to think about.

"Overall, I'm not positive it was Elvis Presley. But I know that people have seen him, and a lot of people are positive. I don't see why I couldn't have seen him too."

It was the holiday season in 1989, and Cindy was finishing up her shift at the bar. The night had been busy but fun. A holiday celebration was going on, and the patrons were friendly and generous, in keeping with the season.

Despite the fun she was having, Cindy was tired and wanted to go home. She began to say good-bye to the regular customers, exchanging holiday wishes with them, when she noticed a man sitting alone at the end of the bar. She felt sorry for him, sitting by himself when those around him were sharing good times, and thought she'd talk to him for a while, despite her desire to go home.

He hesitated a little to speak at first, but he warmed up to Cindy soon enough. She had difficulty seeing his face, as he sat at the darkest end of the bar, but it was somehow familiar. Of whom did it remind her? She tried to recall, but it eluded her at the time.

They continued to talk, and the conversation turned to entertainment. They discussed music for a while, when the man said that one of his best friends was the singer Tom Jones. Cindy found this a bit hard to believe.

At last Cindy said good-bye to him and was about to leave. But there was a nagging question in her mind: Whom did he look like? She decided to turn on a bar light to get a better look at him. She went behind the bar to turn on the switch, but when she turned around to look at him, he had left. It was only then that she realized he looked like Elvis Presley.

Her suspicions were confirmed later, when two men told her they had seen a man entering a stretch limousine outside the bar. Cindy has no doubts about whom she spoke to that holiday season.

SAVING A LIFE

Wade liked to drive fast. Sometimes it got him in trouble. One time it got him a lot more than that.

He was tearing along in his pickup, screeching around the turns on a back road in the Tennessee hills. This was his favorite kind of driving: a little reckless, a hint of danger. It wouldn't take much to go careening off the road down the steep hillsides. If he went a little too fast or cut a turn a little too sharply, he'd miss it and that would be the end of it. There'd be nothing to stop him but the trees.

Wade knew about the risks well enough. He'd seen a few cars that went over. Usually it was because someone was driving drunk late at night. Wade was never that foolish. His problem was an unstoppable thrill-seeking urge. If it was risky, Wade would do it.

He loved everything that posed a danger. He'd go on white-water canoe trips every chance he got. He liked rock-climbing, getting way up high where nothing stands between you and a broken neck but a half-inch ledge your toe is trying to grip. When bungee-jumping started, Wade was one of the first ones to try it. One thing he hadn't done was skydiving, though he always said he'd do it before he died. His friends would usually respond by saying something like, "You'll never live long enough to do it." Or sometimes: "Before you die? That'll be *how* you die! You're such a fool you'll probably jump without a parachute just because it'd be more exciting."

Nothing was fun for Wade unless it involved a risk, even driving these back roads. Fact was, he was going well out of his way on these roads. He could have taken the major highways to get to where he was going, but whenever he had time to spare he'd travel off the beaten path. You couldn't get this kind of fun on the highway.

It was a great day for driving, warm and bright. Wade had his windows rolled down, country music tapes on the stereo, and a road all to himself. It might have been the combination of these things that had him pushing his luck a little more than usual. He took the turns at speeds that were truly dangerous. It wouldn't take much: a little loose gravel on the road, an animal jumping out at him. Any kind of distraction or interference would be a disaster. Wade left no margin for error as he screeched around the bends, whooping as he went.

When even a little disturbance would be trouble, there was no way Wade could handle the blowout. His front tire exploded as he was at the crest of a curve. The truck went completely out of control and sailed off the road, crashing through trees and brush. It careened down the hillside, flopping over onto its back. Wade, who never wore a seat belt, was bounced around like a rag doll. Lucky for him, the woods were pretty thick at that point, because the truck didn't fall too far. A little bit farther and he might have fallen off a small cliff that was ahead and crashed into the stream below it.

When the truck finally stopped, Wade just sat there for a moment. He was such a thrill lover that for a while he couldn't decide if he was upset about what happened or if it was the most fun he'd ever had. The terrible pain in his leg made him decide it wasn't that much fun after all.

He wasn't sure, but it felt like his leg was broken. It had got twisted under the seat as the truck tumbled over, and it took a severe blow. Broken or not, it hurt like hell.

It was the pain that made him realize the gravity of his situation. He had fallen about forty or fifty feet down a steep hillside, and his leg was broken. Chances were that nobody would come along anytime soon, not on these lonely roads, so his chance of getting help was slim. He was faced with the task of climbing back up the hill with his bum leg, and then limping off until he found somebody to help him. This was less fun all the time.

There was nothing to do but get going. Getting out of the truck proved a trial in itself. The truck leaned on one side, so he had to work himself over to the other door and try to push it open. It had been banged up pretty thoroughly and opening it wasn't easy, especially since he had only one leg for leverage. Finally he managed the door and he tumbled out of the truck.

The road didn't seem too far away, so he figured it wasn't going to be too tough. *Just stand up and drag myself up to it,* he thought. It all seemed so simple until he tried to stand up.

Wade had never broken a leg before, despite all his risky activities. He thought it was just a matter of not placing too much weight on it and relying on the good leg. He wasn't prepared for the intense pain that resulted from even a little pressure. When he tried to stand, it was so unbearable that he dropped to the ground screaming. No way could he walk up that hill alone. He'd have to crawl up.

Suddenly, the road seemed miles away. But Wade was no quitter. He grabbed the closest branch and began to haul himself up. For the first five or six feet things went well, but the hill took a sharp upward turn at that point. He got a few feet farther when he lost his grip and slid back down. He ended up nearly where he started. It had taken him half an hour and he had traveled only two feet from the truck.

For the first time in his life, Wade began to know real fear. He had no provisions with him, no food or water. At the rate he was going it would take all night to reach that road. The pain in his leg grew worse all the time. He might pass out before he got to the top of the hill. What would happen then? Would anybody notice him down there? Or would he just die of thirst or shock before someone found him?

Earlier, he had considered yelling, but he didn't because he thought he'd make it up the hill with no trouble. Now he realized how foolish he had been. It was time to yell.

"Hello! Anybody there! I need help! Is anybody there?"

He had a loud voice, but it was hard to yell lying on the ground, and his voice seemed tiny to him, a feeble peeping noise hopelessly trying to rise over the hill. It was breezy, too, and the noise of the leaves swaying nearly drowned out whatever sound he could make. He waited for a few minutes, but nobody came. He hadn't really expected anyone.

Wade knew what these roads were like. It might be days before anyone came along. And then who knows if they would notice anything? The truck was too far down the hill to be seen from the road. What was he going to do?

Well, one thing was sure; he wasn't going to lie there and die. If it took all night to crawl up that hill, then, dammit, he'd crawl all night.

He started up again, but the same thing happened. As soon as he reached the steep part, he couldn't get any farther. He'd try, but he always fell back down. After three attempts, he knew it wasn't going to work. He'd have to work himself sideways until he reached a less steep part of the hill. The trouble was, there didn't seem to be any such part.

Then he got an idea. The horn! He'd honk the truck's

horn over and over. That sound would carry a lot farther than his voice. Somebody was bound to hear it.

His problem was getting back into the truck. It wouldn't be easy to drag himself back into the door he had climbed out of. And the driver's side door was jammed into the ground. There was no way to get that open. He'd have to do what he could.

He propped himself up on the truck and hopped along until he reached the door. Using his good leg for balance, he hauled himself up and let himself flop into the cab. His broken leg banged against metal on the way in, and he screamed out in pain. It hurt so badly that he felt himself losing consciousness, but he fought it off. At least this time. He didn't know how many more shots like that he could withstand.

Things had actually gone well to this point. He made it into the truck fairly easily. Now for the horn.

Thank God, it worked. He was worried that it might have been damaged in the fall, but it sounded out loud and clear. What a sound it was. He'd never heard anything so sweet before.

He honked and honked and honked. For almost an hour, he just let the horn blast, over and over. But he didn't want to use up all his battery power, so after a while he let it rest. He ought to allow someone time to get there and find him.

He sat there, hunched up in the truck, honking every ten minutes or so to help lead any rescuers to him. But time passed, and nobody came.

Wade started to panic. For a few minutes he lost control, letting the horn blast nonstop while he screamed and screamed. Then he heard a horrible sound: the horn was dying. It grew fainter and fainter, and then there was no sound at all. *That's it*, he thought, *I'm dead.*

He started to cry. Wade hadn't cried since childhood, but staring death in the face was too much for him. He loved to face death as long as it kept its distance. Wade wasn't so much brave as incredibly confident. He never believed anything would go wrong. That's what gave him the nerve to climb sheer rock walls or jump off bridges with nothing but a giant rubber band for safety. But now it was different. This time death had the upper hand.

He might have given up at that point and settled down to die, but his own embarrassment saved him. When he realized he was crying, he felt so ashamed of it that it snapped him out of his hysteria. His shame turned to anger, and that motivated him.

Get killed because of a little hill and a broken leg? Not a chance. Wade had handled bigger obstacles in his day. A hill wouldn't beat him.

His bravado was necessary to get him going, but it didn't do anything to improve his situation. The road remained just as far away as ever, and the broken leg hurt intensely.

Gritting his teeth, Wade again navigated his way out of the truck. He dragged himself up the hill, reaching the point where he had always fallen back. He started to pull himself up, when he suddenly stopped. A car! He heard a car!

"Help! Help me!" he screamed. He screamed louder than he ever had in his life, screamed until his lungs burst. Thank God, the car was stopping!

He continued to cry out. "Down here! I'm down here! Help me, please!"

He heard the car door slam. Then a man appeared, looking down the hill at him.

"Are you all right?" the man cried out.

"I'm OK. But my leg's broken and I can't climb out of here. It's too steep."

"Just hang on fella, I'm coming right down."

Wade let his head drop to the ground.

"Thank you, God, thank you," he said, over and over.

He looked up and saw the man moving carefully down the hill.

"Better be careful," Wade called out. "It's pretty steep."

"You're telling me?" the man replied. "Brother, I can tell that much!"

With all his pain, Wade had to laugh. And why not? Help had arrived. He would be saved.

It took some time, but the man reached him. He was a dark-haired man, wearing gold-rimmed glasses. Wade couldn't help but notice that he bore a striking resemblance to Elvis Presley. But it was just a passing thought. He was in no shape to wonder about it.

"How you doing, son?" the man asked.

"I'm in a lot of pain," Wade replied. "But I think I could make it up if I had some help."

"What's your name, son?" the man asked.

"It's Wade. What's yours?"

"John. But never mind that. It's getting late. If it gets dark, we'll have a hell of a time getting you out of here."

John surveyed the situation for a moment.

"Can you stand up at all?" he asked.

"It's not easy, but I can manage."

"All right. Here's what we'll do then. We'll get you up, and I'll help you over that way." He pointed to the right. "It looks a little less steep over there, and the way seems clearer. Once we get there, we've got to get up. It's not going to be easy."

"Don't worry about me," Wade said. "I'll do whatever it takes. I've been down here so long I'm mad as hell at that hill. Let's take a crack at her."

"I like your spirit, Wade. I hope your good leg is strong."

John helped Wade up, and together they walked across the steep hillside. It was rough going, even though they weren't going up. Wade had lost more strength than he thought.

They reached their first goal.

"Let's stop and rest a minute," John said. "But not long. The sun's already starting down."

They caught their breath. And then it began—the slow, agonizing climb.

Wade draped his arm over John's shoulders. He kept his broken leg off the ground as much as possible, but it frequently dropped to the ground, sending sharp jabs of pain through his body.

John held one arm around Wade's waist. With his other arm, he grabbed for handholds to pull them both up. Their progress was agonizingly slow. After an hour, they were only halfway up the hill. It was noticeably darker.

"We've got to speed it up," John said.

"I don't think I can go any faster," Wade said. The pain made him dizzy. He was also desperate for water.

"I'm so tired. So thirsty," he said.

"Thirsty? Why didn't you say so before. Stupid me, I should have asked you that. I've got some water in my car."

John told Wade to hang on to a tree, while he scrambled up the hillside. It was not much trouble on his own. A few minutes later he came back with a bottle of spring-water. Wade drank nearly all of it. He would have finished the bottle but John stopped him.

"Hold on there," he said. "Don't drink too much at one time. You don't want to cramp up or get sick on us.

"Now listen," John continued. "We've got at most half an hour before it gets too dark to see in these woods. Whatever pain you're in, you've got to forget it, understand? We've got to get up that hill. You've got to push yourself like you've never done before. Are you ready for it?"

Wade closed his eyes and breathed deeply.

"Yeah," he said. "I'm ready to go."

"Then let's do it," John said. "Scream if you want to. It might help you go faster."

Then they started. They moved twice as fast as they had

moved earlier. The hill started to flatten out ever so slightly now, leveling enough to make it easier on them. But John was the main reason they made it. He hauled Wade up that hill with tremendous strength. He was sweating and gasping for air, but he wouldn't quit.

They were only a few feet from the top. Both men were exhausted, sucking in gulps of air. Neither could speak for a few moments.

"One more shot," John said. It was nearly dark.

"Ready, Wade?"

Wade nodded.

"Let's go!" John screamed out with his final effort. Wade joined him. Together, both men scrambled up the final few feet, a couple of screaming, dead-tired men fighting together to beat the hill. They lurched over the top and dropped onto the level roadside.

For ten minutes, John and Wade lay there, catching their breath, fighting the pain in their bodies. At last Wade managed to speak. Still lying down, he threw his arm over John's shoulder.

"Thank you, John. You saved my life. I would've died down there. I would've died down there all alone."

"Why it was nothing," John said. "Just a little Sunday walk in the woods, that's all."

Both men started to laugh. It wasn't that John's remark was so funny, it was just a need to release tension. Once they started, it took them a long time to stop laughing. It kept breaking out.

"Stop, stop!" Wade giggled. "It hurts. It hurts when I laugh!"

John broke into hysterics at this. "I'll bet it does!" he said, and they both laughed even harder. Eventually, it died down.

"We've got to get going, Wade. You need to get to a doctor with that leg of yours."

"The closest one's about fifty miles from here."

"No problem. We'll get you into the backseat of my car and we'll be on our way."

With John's help, Wade got into the backseat. Luckily, it was a large car with plenty of room for Wade to lie down. John propped up his leg with blankets so it wouldn't move. It helped the pain if he kept the leg still.

They set off. It was now nighttime.

For a few minutes they drove silently. Then John spoke.

"So what happened? How'd you end up down that hill?"

"My tire blew out."

"Is that all?"

"And I was driving like a fool, I guess. Going too fast."

"I thought so. I could tell. That's how I found you."

"Didn't you hear the horn?"

"Horn? No. I had the windows shut and the radio on. I couldn't hear a jet plane landing on the roof inside this car. But I saw the broken trees where your truck went off the road. I almost passed them by, but something made me check it out. Lucky for you I did."

"I want to thank you again, John. You saved my life. And you took a risk yourself doing it. You could've been hurt trying to get me up that hill."

"That never entered my mind. Not when I saw you down there and you said your leg was broken. One way or another I was going to get you up from there. But it's nothing more than any decent human being would have done."

"That was more than just decent, John. It was a lot more than just decent."

They were silent for a time. Wade drifted in and out of sleep. Then John asked him a strange question.

"Wade, can I ask you a question?"

"You can ask my anything you like."

"Did you think you were going to die? Did you believe you were?"

"For a while I did. It went back and forth. I'd feel hopeless for a time, but then I'd get angry and determined to make it. But I think deep down I always knew that I could never make it by myself.''

''What did it feel like?''

''What did what feel like?'' In his exhaustion, Wade was having some trouble keeping up with things.

''What did it feel like to be looking at death that way?'' John asked again. ''To be so close to it?''

Wade had to think for a minute. ''It's hard to say,'' he began. ''It's scary, there's no question about that. I don't mind saying I was terrified. I didn't want to die, especially down there, all by myself, not knowing if I'd ever be found.

''But there was more to it. Somehow, being so close to death made some things clearer. When I'd snap out of my panic, I had this tremendous concentration. For a while, there'd be nothing in the world but that hill and me. I was so focused on it, it was amazing. I think if I could focus like that all the time, I could pitch a no-hitter every night, or something.''

''Did it help you?''

''It helped me try. Still, there was no way I could make it up that hill alone. Not with my leg like this.''

''Did the concentration go away?''

''Oh sure. It would only last a few minutes. I can't really explain it to you. I've done a lot of things in my life where I have to concentrate hard, like rock-climbing, but I've never been able to focus like I did on that hill.''

''That's very interesting.''

Wade was beginning to wonder why John had such an interest in the way he felt. But his wonder didn't last because his exhaustion overtook him. He drifted off to sleep.

The next thing he knew, he woke up in a hospital room. His leg wore a cast, and an intravenous needle rested in his arm. He found out from a nurse that he had been brought in there the night before by a man who wouldn't identify himself. But the man gave the hospital a thousand dollars in cash and told them to give Wade the best of care. He'd be back sometime the next day.

Now that he had time to think, and his head was a little clearer, Wade began to wonder about John. He looked a lot like Elvis Presley. And thinking about it, Wade thought he sounded like him too. And this money. Who else would give a thousand dollars in cash? Who else would have that kind of money with him? There was nothing to do but wait for him to return.

John came back that evening. Wade wasn't sure what to do. The man, whoever he was, had saved his life. How could he put him on the spot and ask him if he was Elvis Presley? Maybe he'd try to figure it out without asking him directly.

They talked for a while about the hospital and what happened. John explained how he had driven Wade to the hospital and what the doctors had done. At the mention of that, Wade thanked him for the money.

"I can't believe you'd do such a thing for a stranger," Wade said. "But don't worry. I'll send you the money back. My insurance from work will cover most of it anyway. Just give me your address and I'll ship it to you as soon as possible."

"Never mind that," John said. "Really. The money's nothing."

"Nothing? A thousand dollars is nothing? What do you do for a living, John?"

"Me? Well, I . . ." It was clear that John was hesitating, trying to think of an answer.

"Well, I'm in entertainment."

Wade felt funny probing into this, but he couldn't resist.

"You mean like you're a singer or something," Wade said. He thought John looked nervous.

"No, not a singer." *The denial was too quick,* Wade thought. *He's covering up.* "I'm more of a manager."

"Who do you manage?"

"Some singers."

"Like who? I'm interested."

"I'd really rather not say, Wade. For business reasons."

Business reasons? Wade thought that was a poor excuse for an answer. He felt more and more certain that the man was Elvis Presley. Despite his mixed feelings, he had to ask.

"John, tell me something. Are you Elvis Presley?"

John looked at him with wide eyes. He didn't say anything, but he turned his face to the floor.

"Don't worry if you are," Wade said. "You saved my life. I'm not going to tell on you. I'm not going to start screaming your name or anything. I wouldn't do that anyway, and I'm sure not going to do that after what you did for me."

John looked up at him. "I hope you can keep a secret," he said. "I am Elvis Presley."

Wade stared at him. "Good God, you're supposed to be dead."

"You're supposed to be dead, too!" Elvis tried to joke about it. Wade knew he wouldn't get far with this subject, so he dropped it.

"Nah. Forget it. There's a million things I'd like to ask you, Elvis, but I guess it's none of my business. It's enough that you pulled me up that hill. What more can I ask of you?"

"I appreciate that, Wade. I really do. There's a lot I'd like to tell you. A lot I'd like to tell anybody. But I can't just yet. Maybe someday soon. I can't say. But for now, let's just let it go."

"Sure thing."

"And I'd better be going now," Elvis said. "I shouldn't stick around one place too long. It's dangerous."

"Well I'm glad you were in one place long enough to save my life."

"I'm glad I could too. There's not much good I can do for people these days. I used to be able to make them

167

happy with my music, but for now I'm denied that. At least I was in the right place to help you.''

Elvis started to go.

"Elvis!" Wade called to him. "Can I ask you one more question? I can't help myself."

"I won't guarantee an answer, but you can ask.''

"What were you doing on that road?''

Elvis smiled at Wade. "That's one of those things I can't tell you. Now I gotta go. Take care of yourself, Wade. And don't drive so damn fast anymore.''

"Good-bye, Elvis. And thank you again.''

Wade watched him go. There was nothing he could do. He couldn't even follow him, not with a cast on his leg. He was glad when the nurse came and gave him a sleeping pill. All the thoughts flying around in his brain were giving him a terrible headache. He took the pill and drifted off into sleep.

The next day, Wade's sister and some friends arrived at the hospital. They were talking to him, listening to him explain the story. He wasn't saying it was Elvis. He told them he didn't know the man's name. Just a passing Samaritan, he said.

Then one of Wade's friends got the idea of signing his cast.

"Good idea,'' Wade said. "I hadn't even thought of that. You can be the first one.''

They pulled the blankets off his leg. Wade's friend Henry was about to sign.

"I thought you said I'd be first,'' he said.

"You are first,'' said Wade.

"No I'm not. Somebody's already written here.''

"Go on,'' Wade said. "Where?''

He leaned up and looked at the cast. In small letters, Wade saw the words "Slow down'' and "Good luck'' written. It was signed "John.'' The name was in quotation marks.

"Who's John?'' Wade's sister asked.

"Oh, just somebody from the hospital," Wade said. "Just somebody who helped me out."

"Is that all you know about him?" his sister asked.

"Oh, I know a little bit more," Wade said. "I know a little bit more. But it's not important."

ON THE STREET

Chicago, Illinois.

Devon L. and his friends were standing around on the corner, late one November night. The air was icy as it blew down the streets of this tough, urban neighborhood. In order to keep warm they lighted a fire in a garbage can, tearing up some old crates and boxes from a nearby junk pile.

Devon and his friends—Jackie, Donald, Garrett, and Owen—were unusual for this part of town, because they weren't doing anything illegal. Most of the people who dared to step out late at night were troublemakers. It wasn't safe for anyone else.

But Devon and his buddies—they called themselves the Cool Notes—were a fixture on this corner, where they stood almost every night, singing songs. Everybody knew they were there, and they had a kind of immunity from the local toughs. Once in a while somebody would hassle them, and then the Cool Notes would walk away and call it quits for the night. Sometimes if someone was looking to start trouble with the Cool Notes, they would find themselves up against the street gang that made its headquarters in the building on the opposite corner. It was well understood in the neighborhood that the Cool Notes were off-limits.

Devon was a middle-aged man who had lived in the neighborhood all his life. He worked at a civil service maintenance job during the day. He lived alone, his wife having left him years ago when she started earning enough to get out of that part of town. The other guys were much like Devon. They all held low-paying jobs, and they were lifetime residents. There weren't many like them left. Most of those who could afford to had moved away long ago.

The Cool Notes stayed, determined not to give up on what had once been a nice place to live. Somehow, with no real evidence for their beliefs, they all had faith that the neighborhood could come back. So they remained there on the corner, a throwback to a simpler, kinder world, and they sang their own songs, the songs from their youth.

Though they were rarely troubled, they were endlessly made fun of by the young people who laughed good-naturedly at their music. "Sing some rap!" they would shout at the Cool Notes. The singers took it in stride, sometimes giving back as good as they got. And they kept on singing their soulful songs, not caring that music of their sort had long since ceased to be popular.

Tonight they were singing old Sam Cooke songs: "Another Saturday Night," "Sixteen," "Chain Gang," making them all slower than originally, because it sounded better slow out on the street, and it filled up the long, cold night.

They had just started to sing "Cupid," when a stranger turned the corner and came toward them. They stopped singing and stared. It was a white man, not something they saw very often on that corner. Normally, if a white person came by he would be in an expensive car, looking to buy drugs. During the day there were social workers, inspectors, and other whites who worked in the area, but at night it was a rare sight.

"Excuse me," Devon called to him, as the man got closer. "Are you lost?"

"No, I don't think so," the man replied.

"Well, I think you'd better think again. How long do you expect to last out here? Do you have any idea where you are?"

"Well, not really, no, I don't. I just felt like taking a little walk. The streets seemed pretty empty, so I didn't think it would be a problem."

"A problem?" Owen chimed in. "Mister, you are looking for a hell of a problem. How far do you think a well-dressed white guy like you is going to get before some drug nut cracks you over the head?"

"I didn't realize it was dangerous."

"Dangerous? Brother, you don't know."

"But how come you fellas are out here if it's so dangerous?"

"We're special," Devon said. "We're here every night. We're sort of protected in the neighborhood. But you're not. So I'd advise you to get out of here whatever way you came in."

"Yeah, where did you come from anyway?" Garrett asked.

"I came in my car. There it is."

The man pointed to a large black limousine that had turned the corner and waited at the curbside. As he did so, the front passenger door opened up and a large black man stepped out. He was holding his right hand inside his jacket, as if he were reaching for a gun.

"Is everything all right?" he called out.

"Sure is," the stranger called. "I'll be there in a while. Just wait for me."

"OK, but I'll be watching everything," the man said, glaring at the Cool Notes, as if to warn them to watch their step.

"Well, he's thinking who he is," Owen laughed. "Hey, man, you always walk around followed by guys like that?"

"Most of the time I do."

"No wonder you can walk around in this neighborhood."

Then Jackie spoke up.

"What's your name, Mr. Limo?"

"His name?" It was Donald answering. "What do you think it is? Take a look at him. He looks like Elvis Presley."

"Man, you're right, he does," Devon replied. Then they all spoke up at once, asking if he was Elvis Presley, joking and kidding about it.

"It's true, it's true," Elvis replied. "I am Elvis Presley."

"Oh yeah, sure you are," Devon said. "And I'm Jackie Wilson, and this is Sam Cooke, and this is Otis Redding . . ." He broke off in laughter.

"If you're Elvis Presley," Owen said, "why don't you sing a song with us? That's what we do out here."

"I know," Elvis said. "I heard you singing 'Cupid' as I turned the corner. You sounded pretty good."

"Why don't we pick it up with that again?" Donald said. "You sing lead, Elvis."

"Fine with me. I always did like Sam Cooke. This isn't the best song for my kind of singing, but I'll try it."

After a few more moments of chatter, the Cool Notes settled down, set the pitch, and started to sing background. Elvis joined in and did what Devon remembers was a decent job of singing "Cupid," but Elvis was right: his voice wasn't fit for the song, and it came out a bit strained.

"Not bad," Jackie said. "But I'm still not buying that you're Elvis."

"Let's sing an Elvis number," Donald said. "That's the only fair way to test him out."

The Cool Notes argued among themselves over what

song to sing. Finally, they settled on "Too Much." It offered the right kind of beat, one they could snap and hum along to. And it was a song from the fifties, which the Cool Notes always preferred.

"It's been a while since I've sung that one," Elvis said. "But I'll give it a try. I hope I remember all the words. Help me out if I miss any."

The Cool Notes picked up the beat. Elvis hit the notes right on target. He sang far better than on "Cupid," dipping and dodging with the notes, playing off the Cool Notes' backup. It was a great number. A few passersby had stopped to watch, their attention grabbed by the presence of the stranger. When it was over, they clapped for the street corner singers.

High Fives were exchanged all around. The Cool Notes asked for another song.

Just then, the limousine honked its horn.

Elvis turned toward it. The powerful-looking man who had spoken earlier was waving from the window, signaling Elvis to come over.

"Sorry, fellas," he said. "But I really have to get going. It was fun singing with you."

"Stop by and do it again some night," Devon said. "We're always here."

"I don't know if I'll be back this way again for a while," Elvis said. "If I am, you can be sure I'll stop over."

He walked over to the limo and got in the backseat. It pulled into the street quickly and drove away.

The Cool Notes watched it go.

"So what do you all think?" Devon asked. "Was that guy really Elvis Presley?"

"Get out of here, man," Jackie said. "Elvis Presley died ten years ago. It wasn't him."

"Then who was it?" Devon said. "Who else could it be?"

"Just some guy who thinks he's Elvis," Donald said.

"Yeah but driving in a limo? With an armed guard? How many people can do that?"

"So it's some crazy rich guy," Garrett said. "He's just some rich Southern boy who convinced himself he's Elvis Presley, so he goes around singing like him."

"He sang a lot like him," Devon said.

"Yeah, yeah, yeah," Owen chided him. "You go on thinking it was Elvis Presley if you like. But it's getting too late and too cold for me. I'm going home."

The other Cool Notes followed. Devon stayed behind a moment on the corner. He couldn't shake the idea that it was really Elvis Presley. The singing had been so perfect. Devon remembered Elvis's old songs very well. *Nobody could sing it like that,* he thought, *nobody but Elvis.*

"Oh well," he said to himself out loud. "Maybe it was, maybe it wasn't. I guess I'll never know."

That said, he pulled his coat collar tightly around him, shook his head one last time in wonder, and headed home, keeping his face down to avoid the cold night wind.

A DAY AT THE FAIR

Denton, Texas.

Sheila R. knew right away it was Elvis. There wasn't a doubt in her mind. But there was nothing she could do about it.

It was a hot summer day in Denton, and Sheila and some friends went to a carnival to enjoy the weather. They had played some games and gone on a few rides, when Sheila's friend Matty pointed out the parachute ride.

"You'll never get me up on that," Sheila said. She liked fast and frightening rides, but a parachute drop was too much.

But Sheila could never resist a dare, and Matty and the others dared her. Reluctantly, she went along, but she thought she'd regret it. She never could have guessed how much.

She sat down and was strapped in. The ride began to hoist her hundreds of feet into the air while her friends laughed and waved from below. She was as frightened as a lightning-struck hound in a thunderstorm, but she didn't want Matty and the others to see her turning chicken. She tried to keep a calm face. Looking down made everything worse, so she looked straight out. That didn't help much, so Sheila started looking up. All of a sudden, she forgot all about the parachute ride.

About thirty feet above her, she saw him. It was Elvis. He wore dark glasses and had less hair than in pictures, and he was wearing a foolish-looking false moustache, but it was he. She knew. Sheila was a big Elvis fan. She'd heard the stories about people seeing him. She had always hoped she'd run into him one day.

She had the whole moment planned. She'd go to him slowly, not drawing any attention. "Mr. Presley," she'd say, "don't be alarmed. I know it's you, but I won't make a scene. I just want to tell you that I love you, and your fans love you, and we need you back. Please come out of hiding soon, Elvis. The world needs you." Then she'd grab a quick kiss off his cheek and let him go. Sheila always believed that something deeply troubling must have sent Elvis into hiding. She didn't want to bring him any more suffering. She wouldn't even ask for an autograph or a memento, though she'd have killed to have one.

And now there he was, up above her on a parachute ride. He was just about ready to drop. But Sheila was stuck. There was no way for her to go any faster or get any closer. What could she do?

Should she call out to him? No. Not that. At a crowded carnival it could bring hundreds of people running. Elvis would hate that. She wouldn't do it to him. But how could she do nothing? Sheila felt she'd explode as all these thoughts ran through her mind. Then it was too late.

Elvis dropped past her. She saw his parachute open up and slowly lower him to the ground. Sheila was frantic. She had to meet him. But where to go! The only way out was to jump off! She had to ride it out and hope she could find him back on the ground.

It seemed to take forever. Seconds dragged on like hours. Elvis was dropping farther and farther away from her and she was still going up. Finally, she reached the top. Sheila dropped, but it only slowed her more when her parachute opened. She was yanking down on the cords trying to fall faster, but it did nothing. Below her, she saw that Elvis had reached the ground. He was walking away!

She tried to follow him with her eyes. He walked out the ride's gate where three other men met him. The four men walked off to the right, then turned right again, going away behind Sheila. She tried desperately to turn around, but the seat blocked her view.

What seemed like days later, she got to the ground. Matty and her friend were there. "Are you OK?" Matty said. Sheila looked white as a ghost. She didn't even look at her friends. She just ran out the gate and turned in the direction Elvis had gone. Her friends ran after her, scared and confused. Sheila ran through the crowd looking every which way, but it was no use. He was gone.

Finally, her friends caught up to her and stopped her. They thought she'd had a nervous breakdown on the ride. Matty was hysterical.

"Oh my God, Sheila, what did I do? Why did I make you take that ride?" she cried. "Sheila, speak to me!"

Sheila was in tears.

"Elvis!" she said. "I just saw Elvis! But he got away! He got away!"

The friends all sat down and Sheila explained her story, stopping again and again to control her tears. People came over to ask if she was alright. "Yes," she said. "I was just scared on the parachute ride." She wouldn't tell anyone else. It might set off a crazy manhunt for Elvis. She would never do that to him.

Sheila knew this was her one chance, and it had passed her by. What were the odds of seeing Elvis again? She would relive that parachute ride over and over. If only she had been two minutes earlier or two minutes later! She might have got to speak to him.

But one thing made her happy. Now she knew the stories were true. She had believed them before, but there was always a little doubt in her mind because it was all so fantastic. Not any more. Elvis was alive. Knowing that was the best carnival prize of all.

A CRAZY CAR CHASE

It was a hot summer day in Texas, and Joe was tooling along in his Buick on his way to get lunch. *Something light,* he was thinking. *Maybe a salad and a sparkling water.*

He was headed down a wide thoroughfare, three lanes on each side, when he saw a big, black Lincoln coming in the other direction. Both cars stopped at the same light. The only reason Joe was looking at the car was because he had been thinking of getting a car like that. He missed having a big car like the one he used to have, and he was thinking of trading in his midsize vehicle for a giant cruiser like that one. He admired this new model. It was a great-looking machine.

Then Joe noticed the driver. *Funny,* he said to himself, *that guy looks a lot like Elvis Presley. But what would Elvis Presley be doing driving that car, considering he died a long time ago?*

But did he?

A couple of years earlier Joe had heard all the hoopla about people's saying Elvis was really alive. Some woman in Michigan or someplace, he remembered, had seen him. There were even a few people in Texas who thought they saw him. For Joe, it was all pretty funny. *Nothing but a bunch of bored yokels,* he thought, *making up stories to pass the time.* Joe didn't believe the stories. Not him, a sophisticated marketing man working for a big Texas concern.

But this guy in the Lincoln sure looked like Elvis Presley. *Just the way you'd expect him to look after all these years,* Joe thought. Only a few months earlier Joe had been at a printing expo where manufacturers offered their products for sale. He had spent a good deal of time looking at the high-tech printing products of one corporation. One of their sample portfolios included dozens of pictures of Elvis Presley. The images were fresh in his mind. And this guy . . . Well, what could he say? He looked like Elvis. He looked like nobody *but* Elvis.

The light changed. The Elvis look-alike passed him, giving Joe a clear look. By God, he said to himself, that *is* him. That's got to be him!

He was craning his neck looking back at the car when the honking behind him alerted Joe to the changed traffic light. He started to drive away when an impulse took over.

I'll follow him, he thought. *I'll see where he's going.*

Joe always had an impulsive streak, and occasionally it got him into trouble.

What could go wrong? he asked himself. *After all, I'm only going to see where he goes. I won't attack him or anything!*

Joe had to travel several blocks in the wrong direction before there was an opportunity to turn around. He doubted he would even be able to catch up, but he was never one to quit easily, so he continued to pursue his quarry.

He made the U-turn and sped off in the other direction, as fast as he dared to go. He went a mile or two before he realized the futility of his plans. He'd never find that car.

A Crazy Car Chase

Joe's disappointment made him believe more firmly that it had been the real Elvis. It was a curious aspect of human nature, but very often we believe most strongly the things we just get a glimpse of. This was precisely what went on in Joe's mind, and he burned with anger at his failure to catch up to the black Lincoln.

He made another turn and headed back the way he had come. It was then that he saw the car.

"That's it!" He shouted the words out loud to himself as he saw the Lincoln on the opposite side of the street. It was on line for a drive-through car wash.

He had to get there and fast, but the lights were working against him.

"C'mon, c'mon, change!" he muttered to himself, waiting for the green signal. Finally, he managed to turn around, and he took off for the car wash. Just as he got there, he saw Elvis's car disappearing into the car wash.

Now it was time for Joe to have one of those impulses that he would regret later. It didn't occur to him at the time that all he had to do was wait for the car to come out the other end. His mind was ablaze with one thought: "Get to that car!" And nothing was going to stand in his way.

This very quality made him so effective as a marketing man. Once he had a goal in mind, he reached it, no matter what it took. Unfortunately for Joe, sometimes his single-mindedness prevented him from seeing any other possibilities, and he had tunnel vision big time now.

For a mind in that condition, there was only one thing to do. If a car disappeared into a car wash, and you wanted to see who was in that car, you go after it! Simple. And that's what Joe did.

He jumped out of his car and went running toward the car wash. By the time one of the attendants at the entrance saw him coming, he had picked up a big head of steam. He pushed right past the man who was screaming obscenities at him: "Where the *@!@ are you going!"

Suddenly, Joe hit a wall of water. The high-pressure hoses soaked him in a second. But that was just the beginning. Blinded by the spray, he didn't see the giant cloth washing mechanism that was headed his way. He had turned his back to avoid getting water in his face, when suddenly ten thousand heavy, sopping wet rags slapped him on his back, knocking him to the ground. Who knows what would have happened next if the car wash operators hadn't shut off the system. They ran in and dragged Joe out, one of them still cursing and screaming at him.

The car wash was quickly turned on again. After all, they couldn't leave those people trapped in there. At the sound of the machine's coming back to life, Joe jumped up.

"I've got to get in there!" he said. "I've got to see!"

There were now four attendants there, and they were holding him back, yelling for him to stop, calling him crazy and many other less polite things. At this point, a passing police car saw the commotion and pulled into the station.

When Joe saw the police, he stopped struggling. It was at this point that he realized that all he needed to do was wait at the exit to see the car. He started to break away to run to the exit, when one of the cops grabbed him.

"Hold on there!" he yelled. "You're not going anyplace until we get this straightened out."

What was Joe going to do? How could he tell them that he was running into a car wash to see Elvis Presley? They'd think he was crazy and probably arrest him and have his sanity tested. He was at a loss for words. The police again and again asked, "Just what the hell were you doing running into a car wash?"

All Joe could do was say "I don't know," over and over. He had to think of something soon, because he could see the policemen were getting angry. He surely didn't want to be arrested. But how do you explain behavior like his?

With all this on his mind, Joe had one more blow to absorb. As he stared into space, desperately searching for an excuse, he saw the black Lincoln driving away.

There it goes, he said to himself. *There it goes.*

The black Lincoln.

And that's what gave him his excuse. "Lincoln." It was a three-step mental association that probably avoided arrest for Joe. "Lincoln." That was the first name of a college fraternity friend. The two of them had pledged together, and had gone through hazing together. That was the second connection. One of the things they had to do as pledges was walk into the women's department of a big department store and ask to buy a bra. But they had to ask to try one on to see if it fit. At that time, one of the clerks had called the store security, thinking Joe and Lincoln were dangerous sexual perverts. They got out of trouble by explaining it was all a fraternity initiation that they had to pass. They even got to buy the bras after the security guards had a good laugh. He would try the same sort of excuse, but he would modify it a little because he was too old for a fraternity.

By this time, the patience of the police was at an end.

"One last time I'll ask you," one of them roared at him. "What were you doing in that car wash?"

"OK! I'll tell you!" Joe said. "I'm sorry, but I was too embarrassed to say it before. But I don't want to get arrested so I'll tell you."

He paused for a moment.

"I did it on a bet."

"A bet?" The police officers looked unconvinced.

"Yeah, a bet. My friend said it was impossible to run through a car wash. I said it was possible. So he bet me that I wouldn't do it. I admit it, I'm a jerk when it comes to bets. I fall for everything. So I gave it a try. I guess he was right."

The police were smiling now. They seemed to believe his story.

"So what do you owe him?" one of them asked.

"A case of beer. His choice."

"Tough bet," one of the cops said. "I hope he picks a real expensive beer. Serves you right. You know you could have been killed in there."

"I realize that now," Joe said, trying his best to look ashamed and contrite. Inside he was feeling good, because they had believed his story. There was one more hitch to deal with, however.

"So if this was a bet, where's your friend? Shouldn't he have been watching?"

"Umm . . ." It took only a few seconds for Joe to come up with the excuse this time.

"Well, he drove away when he saw the police car. That's why I was trying to run. I wanted to run after him and stop him."

What an excuse! It was perfect. It explained all his crazy behavior.

The police just laughed again.

"Next time you bet someone," one officer told him, "make sure it's something safe, like betting on a football game. Don't do anything so stupid again, because next time you might find yourself in too deep to get out."

"Yes sir, I'll think twice next time."

The policemen walked back to their car, shaking their heads and laughing.

Well, thought Joe, *this sure gives them something to tell their wives over dinner tonight.*

Dinner. That reminded him. He hadn't had lunch. And he was late for work. And he was soaking wet. What would he do now? How could he go back to work like this? He knew what he had to do.

What's one more little lie? he asked himself. He walked over to a pay phone and called his office. He told his secretary that he had been in a car accident and he'd be a little late. He didn't live far away, so it gave him time to rush home, change his clothes, and make it back to work.

He didn't have time to eat, though, and spent the next several hours with a growling stomach. He didn't tell anybody about Elvis.

Strangely enough, nobody at work asked him why he was wearing different clothes after a car accident. He had prepared a story about tearing his pants on some sharp metal, but nobody seemed to notice.

It was the only thing that went right for him that day.

A KICK IN THE PANTS

Billy loved these oldies concerts. Every year, there was an outdoor concert given at a park near his South Carolina home. A couple of groups would play old time rock 'n' roll, just the way he liked it.

Unfortunately for Billy, he had a bad spot this year. Some unexpected things had come up at home, and he couldn't get to the park early enough to get close to the stage, where he usually sat. This year, he was way back on the outskirts of the crowd. But Billy was a man who took things lightly, so he shrugged it off, spread his blanket on the ground, and sat down with his wife and a big box lunch and got ready to enjoy the music.

The first group was good. They played a wide selection of oldies: Chuck Berry, Buddy Holly, Roy Orbison, plenty more. Trouble was, they didn't do enough Elvis.

Billy was a big Elvis fan, and every year he complained that none of the bands at the concert played enough Elvis. His wife Eileen always said that if they played nothing *but* Elvis, Billy would then complain that they didn't do it right. There was no satisfying him on this point, and Billy knew it himself, but he liked to complain about it just the same.

The second group had begun its set when Billy noticed a man who looked like Elvis Presley. He was even wearing a typical Elvis stage costume. It wasn't Elvis, that much was clear. It must have been one of those Elvis impersonators. Billy just had to talk to him. He waved at him, and the man came over.

"Care to join us?" Billy said. "We got lots to eat."

"Why that's mighty friendly of you," the impersonator said. "My name's Jack Payton. As you can see, I'm a professional Elvis impersonator."

"Yeah, I did notice you was dressed kind of funny!" Billy kidded him.

The three of them then started talking about music. Of course, the conversation centered around Elvis. Billy had always wanted to talk to someone who imitated the King. Unlike Elvis fans who disliked anyone's imitating the King, Billy thought it was a fine idea and a genuine tribute to the memory of the greatest singer of all time.

Jack explained that he used to be a regular singer, but he always sounded a bit like Elvis. On the suggestion of a friend, he tried doing an imitation one night at a show, and it went over very well. Since that time he had stuck with it, and he made a good living working out of three different clubs on different nights.

"What's it feel like," Billy asked him, "to be acting like Elvis? Do you ever start to think you are Elvis?"

"No, never," Jack replied. "First of all, I think I'm a pretty good singer, but I'm no Elvis Presley and nobody else is either. That's my first rule. Some other guys who do this start to think they're better than the King, but they're just fooling themselves. I'm not kidding myself about it. I do this because it's fun and I make a good living at it. And I think I'm pretty good. If I weren't good, I suppose I'd be doing something else."

"Hell," Billy said, "Somebody's gonna do it regardless. It may as well be you as another."

They continued to talk about old songs, about their record collections, about the band that was playing. The second group had finished—"Not enough Elvis songs," Billy said—and the third and final group was setting up.

"I know these guys," Jack said. "I sang with them a couple of times."

"Really?" Billy said. "Say, why don't you go up there and see if you can sing a few numbers? That would be great. I'd love to see it."

"That might not be a bad idea," Jack said. "I could mention my show tonight. Might help bring in some people. Tell you what, Billy, I think I'll go ask them and see if they don't mind."

Billy and Eileen wished Jack good luck, and they said they'd drop in to one of his shows sometime soon.

The band began its set, but Jack wasn't with them.

"I guess they won't let him sing," Billy said to Eileen.

"Maybe he'll come on a little later," Eileen replied. "I don't think they'd just change their whole show."

"Guess so," Billy said, but Eileen knew he was disappointed.

After four songs, the guitarist in the band asked for quiet. He had a special announcement, he said.

"Ladies and gentlemen, as you may have heard, Elvis Presley was recently seen in the area. In fact, he's here today. Or at least we have the next best thing.

"Now joining us for a set of Elvis songs is Elvis impersonator Jack Payton."

Billy was whooping it up, hollering and clapping.

"He looks pretty good!" he said.

The band kicked off with "Return to Sender," and Jack did a fine job, Billy thought. When it was over, the crowd applauded with enthusiasm. They seemed to be enjoying it.

But behind him, Billy heard somebody say, "That's no way to sing that song."

He didn't like hearing his new friend spoken of like that, and he turned around to see who said it. It was another Elvis imitator!

This time, the new Elvis wasn't dressed up in stage clothes. He was wearing jeans and a cowboy shirt, with a big hat pulled pretty far down over his face.

What a strange day, Billy thought. *Two Elvis impersonators at the same time.*

Now Jack was singing "Heartbreak Hotel," and it sounded fine to Billy. But the other Elvis laughed when it was over and said to the man with him, "Now that wasn't so bad, but he still isn't getting it quite right."

This time, Billy decided to stick up for Jack.

"Well now I suppose you can sing it better?" he said to the man.

"As a matter of fact, I can," he replied.

"Are you an Elvis impersonator too?" Billy asked.

"Impersonator?" he said. "I can sing a heck of a lot like Elvis, but I'm no impersonator."

"Maybe you should try it," Billy said. "I hear they make good money if they're any good."

"Money? That's one thing I don't need," the man said.

Billy turned away. *What a strange customer,* he thought.

His wife leaned over and whispered to him, "Billy, don't you think there's something strange about this guy?"

"Strange? Yeah, he doesn't want money. I'd call that strange."

"No, I mean look at him. He looks a lot like Elvis Presley. He doesn't look close. He looks exactly like him."

Billy eyed him again.

"Yeah, so what?" he said to Eileen. "He does look just like him. But what does that mean?"

"And what about what he said? He said he sang like Elvis but he wasn't an impersonator."

Eileen was speaking with great excitement in her voice, though she was keeping it low.

"What are you saying, honey?" Billy said. "Are you saying this guy really *is* Elvis?"

"That's just what I'm saying," Eileen replied. "You've heard the stories, that Elvis isn't dead, that his funeral was a hoax. You even said you believed them!"

"Yeah, I said that, but I don't know if I really meant it. It just sounded like it could be true."

Jack had now finished his third number, a convincing "Jailhouse Rock."

The new Elvis was more pleased with it.

"Now that's more like it," he said. "He just needed some time to warm up, maybe. He really isn't that bad. I'd do it a bit differently, but he's one of the best I've heard."

"See!" Eileen hissed in Billy's ear. "Did you hear that?"

"I heard it. But so what? Maybe this guy's a singer too. What does that prove?"

"Well, you can say what you like," Eileen said. "I think I'm going to ask him."

"Ask him? Ask him what? Ask him if he's Elvis Presley?"

"Why shouldn't I? How can it hurt?"

"You'll look a fool, that's how it can hurt."

"Well what if it *is* him? Then how will I look?"

"Why then you'll . . . You'll . . ." Billy couldn't answer this one. Instead, he tried to drop the subject.

"Aww, honey, just forget it. How could it be Elvis Presley? What would he be doing here anyway, out in public like this?"

"Well . . . you could be right," Eileen admitted. "I guess it would be pretty strange after all."

"Sure it would be. Now just forget about it. You're making us miss Jack's song."

It was Jack's last number, a nicely done rendition of

"Love Me Tender." The crowd gave him a big ovation as he thanked them and left the stage.

Then Billy and Eileen overheard the strange man again.

"I did it better," he said. And he started to walk away.

"That's him!" Eileen said, as she grabbed Billy's arm frantically.

"Ouch, woman!" Billy cried. "Your nails are cutting into my arm!"

"But it's him! It's him! It's Elvis!" Eileen was saying under her breath. "What are we going to do?"

"Do? What the hell can we do? You want to yell it out and start a riot? Just sit still and let me think a minute."

"Think? By the time you finish thinking he'll be gone. I'm going to ask him."

Eileen got up to go. Billy grabbed her hand.

"Don't be a fool, Eileen! Leave it alone!"

"No, I can't miss this chance!" she said, and she took off after him.

"Dern fool woman," Billy muttered to himself. "Gonna make herself look like a jackass."

Eileen caught up with the man she thought was Elvis. She called out to him.

"Excuse me, sir!"

The man with Elvis stepped in front of her and blocked her path. But Elvis spoke to her.

"Yes? How can I help you?"

"I know this sounds crazy, but are you Elvis Presley?"

"Now what makes you say that?"

"Well the way you look, and the things you said."

"Things I said? Anybody could have said those things."

"But you look just like him," Eileen said, her nerves stretched taut as a guitar string.

"Everybody looks like somebody, ma'am."

Eileen was at a loss. If it was Elvis, he wasn't going to admit to anything. If it wasn't Elvis, he was playing around with her and making her look a fool. Maybe Billy was right. She should have just stayed away.

"Oh alright then," she said, blushing deep red. "I'm sorry I was so foolish."

She started to walk away, when he called to her.

"Ma'am? Wait a second, ma'am."

Eileen turned back.

"I didn't mean to be rude with you, but you have to understand something."

He stepped close to her and spoke quietly.

"See, if I am Elvis Presley, and I admit it to you, I run a great risk that you'll shout it out and I'll be found. And I might not want to be found just yet."

"Yes." It was all Eileen could say. Her eyes were like saucers.

"You can understand my situation."

"Yes, I can. Oh, but I won't say anything!" she pleaded.

"You promise me that?"

"Yes, I do. I really do."

"Well, ma'am, let's just say this. I really can't prove anything to you just now anyway. And whatever I say, you can believe it or not believe it as you see fit. But if you think I'm Elvis Presley, if you want me to be Elvis Presley, why then I *am* Elvis Presley."

"You are?"

"Ma'am, I'm whatever you need me to be," he said, putting his hands on her shoulders. "That's what I've always been. That's what I'll always be. It's more than just me now. It's bigger than me. It's out of my control."

"I see." Eileen believed it. She felt as though she had turned into a pillar of salt.

"Well, I'd better go now, ma'am. I appreciate you keeping your promise. And maybe someday it will all make sense. I hope so."

He then turned and started to walk away.

"Wait a minute!" Eileen called out.

Elvis turned back. "I have to go, ma'am," he said, with some urgency in his voice.

Eileen somehow got the words out of her strangled throat.

"I just wanted to say . . . well . . . God bless you. And thank you."

"You're welcome, ma'am."

He tipped his hat, and walked over to his car. He drove away while Eileen stood watching.

"What the hell's going on?" It was Billy's voice. He had come up behind her.

"It was him," she said, breathlessly.

"Him who?"

"Elvis."

"Elvis Presley? The real Elvis Presley? How do you know?"

"How do I know? Why, Billy," Eileen said with a wicked smile, "I just know, that's all."

"Now what does that mean?" Billy said with exasperation. "I swear nothing makes any sense today."

"Don't bother trying to understand it all," Eileen said, with a faraway look in her eyes. "It's bigger than you, Billy. It's bigger than me. It's bigger than all of us."

"Bigger? What's bigger? What in the blazes are you talking about? What's bigger?"

"All of it," Eileen said.

"All of *what?*"

"Oh, never mind, Billy. Never mind. Let's go listen to the rest of the music."

She walked back to their blanket and sat down.

Billy stood there for a minute, just shaking his head.

"Who the hell can ever understand a woman?" he said to himself.

It wasn't until several hours later that Eileen told him the whole story. Billy believed every word of it. And he wore out three pairs of pants kicking himself over and over.

A MOMENT OF PEACE

It was a beautiful late afternoon in Wisconsin on Vern R.'s dairy farm. The cows had just been milked and Vern had a few moments to spare. He was walking over to his house when a car pulled up. It was a long, black car with tinted windows. Rather a strange sight for this part of the country.

The car door opened and a dark-haired man stepped out. He was casually dressed, but Vern noticed he had some heavy gold jewelry on. *Whatever is this about?* Vern thought.

The man spoke. "Excuse me. I noticed you had a sign up that you've got fresh milk for sale. I'd like to buy a little if I could."

"Sure can," Vern replied. "How much would you like?"

"Oh, just a quart or two. It's been so long since I had any that I'm curious to see if I still like it."

Vern motioned him over toward the barn. As they headed that way, Vern introduced himself. The man said his name was John.

197

They entered the barn. Vern took John to the milk tanks and filled two quarts for him. They made small talk about the cows and the farm, nothing special.

On the way out of the barn, John had a question for Vern.

"This is quite a lovely place here," he said. "Would you mind if I took a look around?"

"Suit yourself," Vern said.

John set his milk down and began to walk off to the fields. He was out for about half an hour. When Vern told his wife, Martha, about him, she chided Vern for not being neighborly.

"How could you let him walk off all by himself? You should have at least offered to go with him."

"But he seemed like he wanted to be alone," Vern replied.

"How do you know that?" his wife asked. "Did he say so?"

"Not in so many words. But you can tell when a man wants to be alone."

"Well, I think you should have offered to show him around," she said. "Now why don't you go find him and invite him to supper. It would be nice to have someone to talk to."

"Oh, all right." Vern wasn't thrilled with the idea. He wasn't as outgoing as his wife. He liked to let people be, and he wanted them to leave him alone in turn. His wife, on the other hand, would invite anybody to dinner. She loved to see a new face at the table.

Vern found John sitting under a tree on a small hilltop, watching the sunset.

"It's mighty pretty, isn't it?" Vern said, coming up behind him.

John jumped a little.

"You startled me," he said. "I was so deep in my thoughts that I didn't hear you coming."

"Sorry I startled you," Vern said.

"Aww, that's all right," John replied. "It's a small price to pay for your hospitality in letting me sit out here in your fields. This is such a peaceful place. A man could really find himself out here."

"Find himself?" Vern said, not sure what the conversation was about.

"You know, get to think about his life. There's nothing here but God's great beauty. It's like a balm for a wounded soul."

Vern grew a bit tense at this. He was not one for getting into other people's business, and he was very uncomfortable when strangers took too many liberties and spoke of personal things. He decided to change the direction of the conversation.

"Well, I came out here to tell you that my wife Martha has extended an invitation to dinner to you. It's just plain farm cooking, nothing fancy, but you're welcome to join us."

John suddenly beamed. "You know, there's nothing I'd like more. I would love some good home-cooked food. It's been so long since I had any."

"Well, supper should be ready in about fifteen minutes, so you'd best start for the house pretty soon." With that, Vern took his leave.

A bit later, John came into the house, said hello to Martha, and took his seat at the dinner table. They ate fresh corn, grown on the farm, some fish Vern had caught recently, green beans, fresh biscuits, and salad. By the time they were done, there was nothing left. John had eaten everything. He was enjoying the food so much that he didn't even realize how much he had eaten until supper was over. He tried to apologize for eating so much, but Martha wouldn't hear it.

"The last thing you should be is sorry," she said. "I take it as a great compliment that you ate so much. I just wish I'd known you were coming. I would have baked a pie for dessert."

After clearing the table and cleaning up, the three of them retired to the front porch to have coffee. During dinner Martha had tried to find out some things about John, but he wasn't too specific about his background. When she asked him where he was from he just said, "Down South." When asked why he was in Wisconsin, all he said was "I'm just driving around, seeing the country."

Most of the dinner conversation consisted of John's asking endless questions about the farm. How did things work, what was their schedule like, how were they making out? There was no end to his curiosity. Vern found it a little strange, as usual, but Martha was delighted to answer all his questions.

Out on the porch, John again mentioned the peacefulness of the farm.

"This is the most beautiful place. So quiet. Nothing to bother you. Tell me," he asked Vern and Martha, "are you two happy here with your lives? Pardon me if I'm getting a little personal, but I'm interested."

"Happy?" Vern mumbled, not at all pleased with the direction of the conversation. "I guess we're happy."

"Of course we are," Martha said, playfully slapping Vern's knee. "We've always been farm folk and there's no other way we'd like to live. The work is hard, but I wouldn't trade it in."

Martha saw an opening here. She thought she could finally get John to talk about himself.

"Why do you ask a question like that, John?" she said gently. "Are you happy with your life?"

For a moment or two, John gazed off toward the fields.

"Happy?" he said, with a sad voice. "No. I'm not really happy. I was once, a long time ago. Or I thought I was. But then things got worse and worse for me. For years I went along thinking I should be happy, because I had so much that other people envied, but I just wasn't at peace. Then I ran away from it all. I'm happier now than I was then. But I'm not happy."

"Are you still running?" Martha said, her large heart feeling compassion for John.

"Yeah, I sure am," he said. "I think I'll be running for a long time yet."

"What are you running from?" Martha was still curious, but now she was more concerned than nosy.

"I really can't tell you," John said. When he saw the shocked look on Vern's face, he quickly added, "It's nothing wrong or anything. I'm not a fugitive from the law or a criminal. But there are things in my life that I have to run from."

He saw the confusion on his hosts' faces.

"I wish I could explain it to you," he said, "But I can't do that. I just have to keep running."

After a long pause, John wistfully added, "I wish I could find a place to hide, so I could stop all this running for a while."

It was too much for Martha to take. She had to say what she said next.

"Why don't you stay here for a while? We have plenty of room in the house, now that the kids are gone. We could use a boarder."

Vern looked like he'd seen a ghost. *A boarder?* he thought. *There goes my privacy.* But deep down he felt much the same as Martha. He was just too crusty to admit to it.

John seemed stunned by the offer, as if he didn't understand what Martha had said. "Stay here?" he said. "Here on the farm?"

"Why sure," Martha went on. "There's a nice, big room upstairs you could have. It's got the best view in the house. You could stay on for a while, get some rest, and stop running away from whatever it is that's hounding you so."

201

There were tears in John's eyes. "I can't tell you how much it would mean to me if I could stay here," he said. "Even for only a month or so. It would do so much to help me relax and be my old self again."

"Well then that's settled," Martha said. "Have you got your things with you?"

"They're all in the car," John replied. "Everything I need is right in the car."

"So you move in tonight then," Martha said. "That's wonderful."

"Yes, yes it is," John said. "And don't think I won't help around here. I may not know much about running a farm, but I'm willing to pitch in wherever I might be of use, and I'm willing to learn a thing or two."

"Now that won't be necessary," Martha said.

"No, it is necessary," John said, his voice full of feeling. "Don't you see? That's just what I need. A little hard, honest work, something to take my mind off things. There's nothing I'd like more than to go to bed at night tired out from a long day's work, with nothing on my mind but the sound of the breeze outside my window. Why this is paradise for me."

So things were settled. Martha asked for fifty dollars a week to cover food and lodging, but John insisted on five times that. "You need it more than I do," he said. "The stuff hasn't done me any good in my life; I've got no great affection for it."

He brought only one bag to his room, enough for a change of clothes and something to sleep in. The rest could wait until the next day. Tonight, John just wanted to get into bed and enjoy the peace and quiet. He asked if there was anything to read in the house, and Martha directed him to several ceiling-high bookcases, full of old, hardcover books, mostly classic novels, history, and biography. Martha and Vern were great readers. She was more inclined to the novels, while Vern was the history buff. The Civil War was his particular interest.

"There's plenty of fine reading here," John said. But in the end, he selected the King James Version of the Bible. "Tonight is a night of giving thanks," he said to Martha. Then he said good-night, and went off to his room.

The following day began early for John, as farm mornings always do. It took him a minute to get used to waking up before dawn, but he had gone to sleep early the night before and slept so soundly that he soon felt plenty of energy. The hearty breakfast Martha dished out made him feel that much better.

John followed Vern out to the barn, to see if he could be of any help. While they were there, a tanker truck came along to pick up the milk. John left Vern's side because he wanted to see how the milk truck worked. Vern never saw him again.

About fifteen minutes later, Vern started to wonder where John was. He wanted to show him how the calves were fed, so he went to the house to look for him. He asked Martha if she'd seen him, and she said no. She had been out in the garden and had just come inside.

Then there was a knock at the door. It was Dan, the truck driver from the dairy company.

"Howdy, Vern, Martha," he said. "That sure is a strange fellow you've got there."

"Strange? You mean John?" Vern asked.

"John? Is that his name? I figured it was something else at first."

"What do you mean?" Martha said. She had a funny feeling in her stomach.

"Well when he came over to see the milk pumping, I started to explain to him how it worked. Then I noticed there was something very familiar about the way he looked. He looked just like Elvis Presley."

"Elvis Presley?" Martha asked, startled. *Of course,* she thought, *he does look like him.* Why had she never thought of it before?

"That's just the beginning," Dan said. "I thought I'd joke him about it a little, and I said, 'Say, are you Elvis Presley? I hear tell he's not really dead.'

"I thought he'd take it good-naturedly, but he looked like he was ghost-struck when I said it. He turned all pale and just shook his head. 'No,' he said. 'I'm not Elvis Presley.' And then without saying another word he turned and walked toward the house."

"The house?" Martha asked. "Why then he must be upstairs. I'm going to see about this."

She went upstairs while Dan and Vern remained downstairs chatting. A moment later she returned, looking upset.

"He's gone," she said. "His bag isn't there, and he's gone."

"Gone?" Vern said. "What about his car?"

They all ran out the door, and sure enough, the car was gone.

"Now what do you suppose that was all about?" Vern said, shaking his head. "And I was really growing to like him."

"He left this behind," Martha said, holding up a tightly folded piece of paper. There was something inside it.

She opened it up and found three hundred-dollar bills inside. On the inside of the paper John had written a note. It was very brief.

"Dear Vern and Martha, I am sorry to leave this way, but I have to keep running. If you want to know why, ask the man who picks up the milk. God bless you for trying to help me." It was signed "John."

It seems clear enough to Vern and Martha that Elvis Presley was a boarder in their house for one night. Vern, typically, has little to say about it. Martha, as usual, has more words.

A Moment of Peace

"I feel so sorry for that man," she said. "If only I could reach him I'd tell him he can still stay here. We'd do whatever we could to keep his identity a secret, to let him have some peace. He's a soul in torment, he truly is. It's all so clear now, since I learned who he was.

"Wherever he's gone, I hope he finds someplace he can stay for a while, someplace to rest his heart. It's a long, lonesome road he's on. He may never get to the end of it."

CONCLUSIONS

In the end, it is difficult to know just what to make of all the stories about Elvis presented in this book. There were other stories we could have used, but many were questionable, some obviously fake. It is inevitable that some people will try to create a hoax or win a few moments of celebrity for themselves by claiming to have seen or talked to Elvis. In putting together this book, all possible precautions were taken to weed out stories that didn't ring true.

Some stories were clearly inconsistent with the known personality of Elvis Presley. Some seemed created to make Elvis look bad, to impugn his character in some way. Others were simply bizarre or ridiculous, such as one story of Elvis stepping out of a spaceship, and another having him living in a secret installation at the bottom of the sea.

But most of the time, stories we didn't use were ones that couldn't be explored in any detail. There are literally hundreds of Elvis sightings, some as far away as Korea and Japan, but they are most often reported in one or two lines in a newspaper, and no names are given. Such stories cannot be traced and the details remain out of reach. In any event, the majority of them are probably not true. Were every Elvis sighting a real one, someone would be seeing Elvis nearly every day.

The stories in this book are the ones that seemed most likely to have been real. Of course, we can only write about what people have told us. Naturally, there may be exaggerations in some of the stories. Some took place years before they were retold. Not every detail may have been recalled the way it happened. It is unfortunate, but nothing can be done about people's memories. This is a particular problem with Elvis sightings because very often people do not immediately realize they are in the presence of Elvis Presley, so they are not giving the meeting any particular attention. Remembering everything clearly even a few days later isn't easy, as anyone can see by trying to re-create the dialogue of a week-old conversation.

But what matters is that in all these stories the essence of the meeting is captured. Every bit of dialogue might not be exactly what was said, the finer details may be unclear, but the main events are there for everyone to ponder. Particular care was given when re-creating Elvis's own words. Every possible caution was taken to make sure the precise message, if not the precise words, was brought across.

With that in mind, there are a few things more worth saying. If Elvis is alive—and the evidence of these tales would indicate that he is—he seems to be in good health and likely to continue living for a number of years to come. The biggest question is whether or not he will make himself known publicly. From what we have learned in these stories, it seems that it may happen. On several occasions, Elvis expressed a desire to "come back to life," if we can use such a phrase, but the time is not yet right, for whatever reason. This implies that at some point in the future the time *will* be right and Elvis expects that day will arrive. When that may be we cannot know. We can only hope it is soon.

Personally, Elvis seems to have gained the wisdom of long experience with the world. Very often, his words to people are words of help, words of hope, wise advice, or gentle regret at his inability to stay and talk. He is always friendly, and often takes great risks talking to people who might at any moment turn on him and try to reveal his identity. On some occasions he has been absolutely daring, appearing publicly, even singing. Without question, he longs to return to the world. At times, he seems unable to resist taking a step or two back into normal life, but in the end he always pulls away and returns to his mysterious exile. Whatever is keeping him away from the world must be something powerful and significant because the world is pulling hard to bring him back.

And so the mystery stands. Very little is clear, very little is certain, but between the fateful day of August 16, 1977 and the present lies a great, dark cloud of doubt and wonder. A few shafts of light have pierced that cloud, and a shadowy figure has been seen within, but the cloud always draws itself closed and the figure disappears again into the mists. We cannot understand why he chooses to remain secluded; we don't know when the clouds will part; but we will dare to say this: The King lives. And someday the King will return.

Until then, we have a thousand songs to warm our hearts and a million memories to dry our tears. Where there was once only the sadness of death, now we have the joy of hope, the felicity of possibility. We can do nothing but wait, so wait we shall, for the day when the dark clouds will part and the world will once again greet its great son, the man, the mystery, the forever King of Rock and Roll, Elvis Aron Presley.

If you've seen Elvis, please write to:

Peter Eicher
c/o Avon Books
1350 Avenue of the Americas
New York, NY 10019

The Best in Biographies from Avon Books

IT'S ALWAYS SOMETHING
by Gilda Radner   71072-2/$5.95 US/$6.95 Can

**JACK NICHOLSON: THE UNAUTHORIZED
BIOGRAPHY** *by Barbara and Scott Siegel*
76341-9/$4.50 US/$5.50 Can

STILL TALKING
by Joan Rivers   71992-4/$5.99 US/$6.99 Can

CARY GRANT: THE LONELY HEART
by Charles Higham and Roy Moseley
71099-9/$5.99 US/$6.99 Can

I, TINA
by Tina Turner with Kurt Loder
70097-2/$4.95 US/$5.95 Can

ONE MORE TIME
by Carol Burnett   70449-8/$4.95 US/$5.95 Can

PATTY HEARST: HER OWN STORY
by Patricia Campbell Hearst with Alvin Moscow
70651-2/$4.50 US/$5.95 Can

SPIKE LEE
by Alex Patterson   76994-8/$4.99 US/$5.99 Can

Zecharia Sitchin's
The Earth Chronicles

BOOK I: THE 12TH PLANET
39362-X/$5.99 US/$6.99 CAN

This revolutionary work brings together lost, antediluvian texts, ancient cosmologies, and newly discovered celestial maps to reach the shocking conclusion that we are descendants of a superior race from the 12th planet.

BOOK II: THE STAIRWAY TO HEAVEN
63339-6/$5.99 US/$6.99 CAN

The mysteries of man's pursuit of immortality and afterlife with the gods is researched through the astounding conclusions based on names, places, and monuments whose true meanings have been lost for centuries.

BOOK III: THE WARS OF GODS AND MEN
89-585-4/$5.99 US/$6.99 CAN

Mankind's earliest records reveal a startling new theory of human origins—and of the "gods" who destroyed the first civilization!

BOOK IV: THE LOST REALMS
75890-3/$4.95 US/$5.95 CAN

In the fourth volume of this intriguing study, Sitchin again turns to ancient sources for proof supporting his theories that millennia ago alien visitors shaped our destiny.

Don't Miss the New Companion Volume to
The Earth Chronicles

GENESIS REVISITED: IS MODERN SCIENCE CATCHING UP WITH ANCIENT KNOWLEDGE?
76159-9/$4.95 US/$5.95 CAN